# STRONG
# SUPPLY
# CHAINS

## THROUGH RESILIENT OPERATIONS

SUKETU GANDHI, MICHAEL F. STROHMER, MARC LAKNER, TIFFANY HICKERSON, AND SHERRI HE

# STRONG SUPPLY CHAINS

## THROUGH RESILIENT OPERATIONS

5 PRINCIPLES FOR LEADERS TO WIN IN A VOLATILE WORLD

WILEY

Published by John Wiley & Sons, Inc., Hoboken, New Jersey.
Published simultaneously in Canada.

For general information on our other products and services or for technical support, please contact our Customer Care Department within the United States at (800) 762-2974, outside the United States at (317) 572-3993 or fax (317) 572-4002.

Wiley also publishes its books in a variety of electronic formats. Some content that appears in print may not be available in electronic formats. For more information about Wiley products, visit our web site at www.wiley.com.

*Library of Congress Cataloging-in-Publication Data:*

Names: Gandhi, Suketu, author. | Strohmer, Michael F., author. | Lakner, Marc, author. | Hickerson, Tiffany, author. | He, Sherri, author.
Title: Strong supply chains through resilient operations : 5 principles for leaders to win in a volatile world / Suketu Gandhi, Michael F. Strohmer, Marc Lakner, Tiffany Hickerson, Sherri He.
Description: Hoboken, New Jersey : Wiley, [2024] | Includes index.
Identifiers: LCCN 2023025001 (print) | LCCN 2023025002 (ebook) | ISBN 9781394201587 (cloth) | ISBN 9781394201648 (adobe pdf) | ISBN 9781394201594 (epub)
Subjects: LCSH: Business logistics. | Organizational resilience. | COVID-19 Pandemic, 2020—Influence.
Classification: LCC HD58.9 .G36 2024 (print) | LCC HD58.9 (ebook) | DDC 658.7—dc23/eng/20230712
LC record available at https://lccn.loc.gov/2023025001
LC ebook record available at https://lccn.loc.gov/2023025002

Cover Design: Wiley
Cover Image: © 9bdesign/Shutterstock
SKY10055393_091523

*For our clients, colleagues and beloved ones.*

# CONTENTS

# PREFACE: BUILDING STRONG SUPPLY CHAINS TO PROFIT DESPITE DISRUPTIONS

A company's products, services, strategy, and customers are all important. But the supply chain behind all of this delivers to customers the value they were promised.

Supply chains are receiving a lot of attention, because they were devastated in the early 2020s by the COVID-19 pandemic, labor shortages, social unrest, war, and other shocks. Supply chain redesign enabled globalization, which reshaped the planet and transformed economies. Now, both executives and popular media talk about supply chains as battered and broken. The pandemic unveiled hidden vulnerabilities and showed us that many supply chains are unsustainable.

Why weren't the world's supply chains agile and resilient in the early 2020s? It's a story of too much emphasis on one element. For decades, companies focused on lowering costs. They interpreted *lean* manufacturing principles as primarily reducing costs of labor and other inputs. As they maximized efficiency to take full advantage of economies of scale through globalization, there was little thought for error or for redundancy. They failed to sufficiently realize how much their success depended on stability.

Today, companies operate in a VUCA world: volatile, uncertain, complex, and ambiguous.[1] It's *volatile* because conditions change quickly. Pandemics erupt, wildfires blaze, ports close, neighboring despots invade. It's *uncertain* because at least some of these trends are nearly impossible to predict. Planners prefer certainty—"the part will be here tomorrow at 9:00 a.m."—but management amid uncertainty requires different skills. At the same time, the world is *complex*, with plenty of moving parts, many of them interdependent. Complexity requires backup plans and well-thought-out contingencies. Finally, the world is *ambiguous* because even when information is available, it can be interpreted in multiple ways. You may be tempted to jump to incorrect conclusions.

At the height of globalization, people wanted to believe that the world would always evolve toward stability. But given recent events, it would be naïve to wait for stability to magically return—so leaders should look for a strategy that will win in an uncertain world.

Hence the business world's recent focus on *resilience*, which is the ability to navigate the world by continuously sensing threats and proactively building contingencies. The crisis erupts, the part doesn't arrive on time, the implications ripple out, and the limited available information isn't easily interpreted—but you'll be okay. Your processes, people, and systems were built to handle this. Your operations are resilient.

Resilience applies to all aspects of business, but it's especially relevant to supply chains for two reasons. First, as mentioned, most supply chains were built assuming a stable world—and never reconfigured as markets turned increasingly volatile. "*If you can find a lower-cost supplier, make the change. The risks seem minimal.*" Now we are experiencing some of the risks. They're big: the need for expedited shipments and stockpiling makes costs explode. Stock-outs lead to loss of revenue and loss of customers. Constant firefighting makes employees lose purpose and quit in droves. Now we have learned: if you can effectively address these risks and be more resilient than your competitors, you will gain advantage and win market share.

Second, thinking about VUCA and supply chains highlights the role of *operations*. In the early 20th century, companies had to efficiently arrange their assembly lines and processes on the factory floor. This was the biggest key to their success. It was the age of operations. Then, through 20th-century advances in marketing and technology and an overall increase in prosperity, operations stepped back and focus shifted to enabling demand-driven strategies. "*The product gets made—whatever. Let's talk about how we'll advertise it!*"

Now, we are at the cusp of another pivotal change. The pandemic didn't just disrupt supply chains—it gave a preview of vast disruptions to come. Some firms will navigate those disruptions by optimizing the flow of materials, cash, and information through global networks. Their resilience will provide them with greater profits than they would get by continuing to focus on costs, or advertising, or technology for its own sake.

This is an exciting opportunity for executives. But reaching this level of resilience will require a lot of work. You need new operational strategies. You need to transform your operations to fulfill those strategies. And more than that: you need a new mindset that puts resilient operations at the heart of your company. Operations should shape corporate strategies. Resilience should shape corporate values.

This book will show you how. It discusses core principles, shows how to put plans into practice, and examines how to respond to scenarios of the future. Its insights have arisen from our firm's work with clients, which we have frequently distilled into articles published as part of the Kearney Supply Chain Institute (KSCI). The Notes provide links to more detailed analyses, often specific to an industry or challenge.

The book is anchored in five business principles of resilient operations:

1. Build resilience against supply shocks by empowering your supply base
2. Build resilience against demand shocks by using your operations to create customer value
3. Create resilient teams by leaning into new ways of working and the benefits of diversity
4. Enable resilience through technology by combining human judgment with artificial intelligence
5. Ensure long-term resilience by embracing sustainability

We're not claiming that any of these principles are earth-shatteringly new. Indeed, they've stood the test of time. Now they need to be applied across operations. Finding the right combination of these five principles that works for your specific firm will lead you to resilience and beyond: to operations that are regenerative, and able to recover from any disruption or crises. Thus will you ensure sustained success.

In Part I of this book, we lay out the strategy of how these five principles can be combined to drive your future profitability and growth.

In Part II, we go into more detail on how to implement resilience. For each principle, we provide five actions, from the tactical to the strategic, to bring that principle to life. We provide plenty of examples of real-life firms doing this work. Then in Part III, we look to the future, laying out potential scenarios and showing how the principles can help you thrive despite uncertainty.

When we talk about these business principles, it's not pie-in-the-sky platitudes. And when we talk about business transformation, it's something we ourselves have lived. We all work for Kearney, the consulting firm. The firm's roots go back almost 100 years, to the golden age of operations. Our founder Tom Kearney helped companies address operational issues back then, and he had a reputation for rolling up his sleeves and walking around the factory floor.[2] Tom's successors have been doing the same ever since. We are just the latest generation of operations aficionados, who learn by helping our clients solve real-world problems. This book reflects our accumulation of that learning. We hope you get as much out of reading it as we did writing it.

# PART I

# Five Principles to Transform Your Operations Strategy

If it's not carefully defined, *resilience* risks becoming a meaningless buzz-word. Indeed a prior philosophy, *lean*, came to stand for all sorts of superficial and misapplied pieces of a framework that needed to be applied deeply and holistically. So let's be clear: resilience is the ability to withstand risks. Those risks may come in various forms (supply, demand, internal, external, short term, long term, etc.). So too might the forms of withstanding them (more transparency, better predictions, richer backup plans, quicker decision-making, etc.). But a resilient company will be able to succeed amid tomorrow's risks better than a non-resilient one.

Part I examines the five principles you can use to strengthen the resilience of your operations. Let's start by looking into why operations are so important, and why they're so ripe for transformation.

CHAPTER 1

# Strong Operations Drive Growth and Profits by Adjusting to an Ever-Changing World

The COVID-19 pandemic marked the end of an era. Pandemic effects rippled through supply and labor markets, geopolitical tensions mounted, and the climate crisis increasingly took its toll. We are experiencing the biggest remaking of the global economy since the end of World War II. As with other global rewirings, such as the industrial revolution, the unleashing of the internet, and the move to offshoring, the only thing we know for sure about this new business environment is that it will be less stable than the economic conditions of past decades. External conditions keep changing—and firms' operations struggle to keep up. Businesses are realizing that they need to be more flexible. They need resilience.

## Resilience Across the Value Chain

*Resilience* is the ability to recover quickly from difficulties. Yet in a fast-changing world, you should not recover to some previous state—because the previous state contributed to your disruption in the first place.

The world will never go "back to normal." In the new business reality, there is no normal anymore—only continual disruptions. Thus, businesses need to adapt quickly to any type of difficulty by proactively strengthening all links in the supply chain. To do this, they need a clear operations strategy that combines business, financial, and other strategies. Wider trends are bringing companies back to basics. How do your operations work, and how effectively can they adjust?

This new imperative amounts to a fundamental restructuring of global value chains. "Lean" no longer reigns supreme. The philosophy is still important, especially in its original vision of balancing cost, efficiency, reliability, and resilience.[1] But the old, single-minded focus on *driving down costs* resulted in rigid and brittle operations. To succeed in a post-pandemic world, companies must transform. Supply chains must be more agile. Operations must be more flexible and more sustainable.

The definitions of *operations* and *supply chain* may seem self-evident, but let's take a moment to note their relationship (see Figure 1.1). Your company starts by wanting to sell something to customers in markets. You create products and portfolios, and plan for how to make them. Suppliers make inputs to your manufacturing sites, and then your logistics functions distribute products to customers, ideally with some customer-service follow up. In a narrow sense, the *supply chain* may be only the part between the two middle segments of this figure: suppliers and manufacturing. But

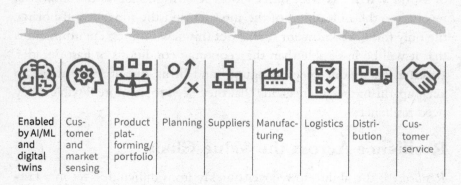

| Enabled by AI/ML and digital twins | Customer and market sensing | Product plat-forming/portfolio | Planning | Suppliers | Manufac-turing | Logistics | Distri-bution | Customer service |

**Figure 1.1**  A holistic value chain includes operations and supply chains
*Source:* Kearney analysis.

really the supply chain, and all of these operations activities, are components of a more holistic *value chain*. To build stronger, more agile supply chains, you can become more resilient at every step in this chain. You can prioritize responsiveness as well as cost and performance.

## Resilience and Competitive Advantage

Operations resilience was not necessarily valuable in the previous globalization paradigm. Then, competitive advantage often arose from customer focus or innovative products. Operations were seen as an enabler of the overall firm strategy, rather than a differentiator: To get the product to the customer as fast as possible and tailor it to their preferences. To get all required inputs to design and manufacture an innovative product. To be as efficient as possible to keep costs low.

Naturally, some firms did leverage operations strategy as a differentiator—often to achieve growth through cost leadership or shorter lead times. For example, in the 1970s, FedEx (then named Federal Express) revolutionized delivery with its then-radical idea to fly almost all packages to Memphis and then back out again. In the 1980s, Toyota engaged in a David-and-Goliath battle with US carmakers, carrying only a slingshot in the form of its unique operational culture. In the 1990s, Walmart promised nationwide consumers everlower prices, trusting that its attention to operations detail would make those prices profitable. In short, operations have previously been a path to profit and growth.

What is different now is that we are experiencing supply chains breaking down on a never-before-seen scale due to intensifying global disruptions. We are moving from a global economy in which supply was generally available toward an economy of scarcity. The critical inputs didn't magically disappear—the new challenge lies much more in the *allocation* of goods. For example, transport systems have broken down due to the pandemic and related labor shortages. In the resulting congestion, critical goods cannot be delivered on time. Trade barriers and import quotas are on the rise as global sentiments become increasingly protectionist. Energy shortages and adverse weather events cause production outages and price hikes around the globe. These effects may eventually drive structural scarcity, rather than scarcity that varies by time and location. But for now, the main result is that global supply markets have become much more volatile.

Can your firm respond to these conditions by creating operations excellence that goes beyond cost optimization? If so, you will secure logistics capacity, identify and develop critical suppliers, and plan for price hikes and supply failures. And you will be able to grow in this disruptive climate, while your less resilient competitors will wither. But only if you spend at least as much effort developing and ensuring supply as you already do developing and ensuring demand.

## Resilience as a Differentiator amid Crises

The 2020s so far have already presented crises in labor, raw materials, logistics capacities, and energy. In early 2020, people hoped that "shortages" would be a simple story involving temporary closures of Chinese factories. But as events played out, the pandemic caused on-and-off closures of factories worldwide—as well as ports, distribution centers, and other essential functions. Supply chains remained in crisis. Soon other crises arrived. The Ukraine war had ripple effects on global flows of grain and natural gas. Increased US-China tensions posed risks to supply bases. And climate change had ever-more-visible, ever-more-devastating effects. Suddenly everything seemed more complex. Semiconductors became impossible to find. The supply chains for rare-earth metals and pharmaceutical inputs clashed with environmental, social, and governance (ESG) goals. Ports became congested, and an entire fragile system became destabilized. Supply chain managers often found creative solutions, but in a world of the *great resignation* and *quiet quitting*, they risked burnout.

Are these accumulating and concurrent crises just coincidence, just bad luck? Just new sets of risks to anxiously track in gigantic spreadsheets? We believe that on the contrary, they indicate deeper problems. Most companies' operations simply were not designed to handle this degree of volatility. And so it's time to change that operating model.

The stakes are high. All companies seek unique strengths to drive profit and growth. Resilient operations are such a differentiator—when implemented at the core of the firm. Since 2020, we at Kearney have seen highly differentiated financial returns for companies that have resilient operations. Specifically, we have worked with companies that have harvested low-hanging fruit, such as product segmentation or operational improvements within warehouses to achieve benefits of a few percentage points of earnings before interest, taxes, depreciation, and amortization (EBITDA). This book can help point you toward such projects, although you may already be familiar with some of them. What we really want to do in this book is put such projects in a wider framework and point out the benefits of moving holistically toward that framework. If you truly transform—as we have seen by supporting companies in broader transformations—you can achieve double-digit EBITDA growth.

How do companies achieve such returns? First, they transform broader corporate strategy. Second, they transform themselves. Third, they transform the careers of the people who drive those changes.

## Operations as the Path to Profits

Many smart chief operations officers (COOs) are already addressing resilient operations. In a 2022 Kearney survey, 56% of leaders considered resilience a top-five priority. Nearly 80% have embedded resilience into their decision-making processes, quantifying it as a key performance indicator (KPI). Nearly 85% are altering their manufacturing footprint by reshoring, nearshoring, and/or offshoring at a granular level. To address inflation, more than half have formed alliances with existing suppliers and embraced design thinking, rather than merely passing price increases on to customers.[2] As Figure 1.2 shows, operations leaders can undertake projects to improve resilience at each step of the value chain.

Why are they prioritizing resilience? You can think about the answer in two ways. First, the pandemic forced firms to rejigger their supply chains on the fly. Now COOs are seeing benefits. So they're seeking to institutionalize the ideals that got them through the pandemic. The

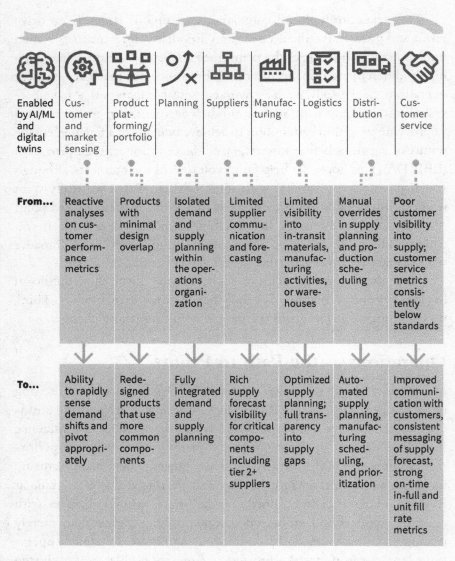

| | Enabled by AI/ML and digital twins | Customer and market sensing | Product platforming/ portfolio | Planning | Suppliers | Manufacturing | Logistics | Distribution | Customer service |
|---|---|---|---|---|---|---|---|---|---|
| **From...** | | Reactive analyses on customer performance metrics | Products with minimal design overlap | Isolated demand and supply planning within the operations organization | Limited supplier communication and forecasting | Limited visibility into in-transit materials, manufacturing activities, or warehouses | Manual overrides in supply planning and production scheduling | Poor customer visibility into supply; customer service metrics consistently below standards |
| **To...** | | Ability to rapidly sense demand shifts and pivot appropriately | Redesigned products that use more common components | Fully integrated demand and supply planning | Rich supply forecast visibility for critical components including tier 2+ suppliers | Optimized supply planning; full transparency into supply gaps | Automated supply planning, manufacturing scheduling, and prioritization | Improved communication with customers, consistent messaging of supply forecast, strong on-time in-full and unit fill rate metrics |

**Figure 1.2**  At every operations step, projects can improve resilience
*Source:* Kearney analysis.

rejiggering created an ad-hoc resilience, but now it's time to drive structural resilience deep into the firm. Second, leaders of the companies that employ those COOs have come to understand that operations are today's path to profits. In other words, they have seen the value of changing not only operations strategy but also the company's values. Consider that by the end of the Cold War, many companies saw that *globalization* was the path to profits. You could move your supply chain to a low-cost country. And you could market your products to newly empowered consumers in newly opened economies. Those moves were worthwhile because they boosted profits. But they were also responses to external changes: newly available labor forces and consumers thanks to the opening of the formerly Communist world. These moves also changed companies' values. Maybe they made you more cost-focused, more aware of shareholder desires to keep expenses down. Maybe they made you more global, better able to pay attention to the varying needs of diverse global customers. Maybe they enabled you to provide opportunities for talented global employees to collaborate. These changes in values were good, and necessary—because they represented your journey on the path to profits.

You're always on a path to profits. Sometimes external changes dictate slight deviations, as in the late 1990s, when the path needed to go through the internet. Sometimes there's a blockage, as in the aftermath of the 2008 financial crisis, when it had to detour through fiscal management. If you didn't adjust your values to these detours—if you tried to operate analog in a digital world or with 1990s bookkeeping in the 2010s—your company would be in trouble. Today's detour is even bigger.

Today's myriad disruptions represent the risks of the globalized world catching up with us. We built our distribution systems without awareness of chaos theory, we built our economic assumptions without sufficient contemplation of how a pandemic could threaten them, we built our transportation and power systems by assuming away the effects of burning all that carbon. But now we (should) know better. Now we know that with a 6% vaccination rate in world's poorest 52 countries, future pandemics are possible (indeed the current one may not be over). We know that ballooning global public debt-to-GDP ratios—at 97% in 2020—could create debt crises or other risks to economic recovery. We know that many countries worry about erosion of social cohesion, especially given the likelihood of exacerbating income disparities. And we know the risks of a changing climate: floods, wild-fires, and other extreme weather events being only the most obvious. If you try to operate lean in this risky world, your company will be in trouble.[3]

However, if your resilient operations mean that you can deliver when your competitor can't, you win market share. Your journey will even take you to unexpected, wonderful places. What might that look like? Some examples:

- You move operations closer to customers, and in that reshoring effort you discover design modifications that save you money.
- You leverage data analytics and artificial intelligence (AI) to bring the voice of the customer throughout your organization and gain the ability to make smarter, quicker decisions.
- You embrace sustainability as a core principle—implementing it across all functions of your company and its supply chain—and discover new sustainable designs that lead to new customers and new growth.

To be successful in such a journey to profitability, you must commit fully to it. You must transform your company with resilient operations at its core. Of course, your journey will be unique to your company. But five core principles describe success in our new VUCA world. You'll probably use some combination of them.

## Five Principles of Operational Excellence

A resilient supply chain can perceive what is happening internally and externally—and quickly and continuously adapt to those conditions. We like to use the phrase *sense and pivot* (see Figure 1.3). First, you sense external signals: maybe demand is shifting, maybe supply is becoming scarce. Then, you pivot internally: you adapt your plan and strategy on the fly to better fit the new reality. You're performing against both your plan and the unplannable. Your dynamic responses make you adaptable. At the same time, you're improving your capabilities to digitize and automate, improving the speed and efficiency of your response.[4]

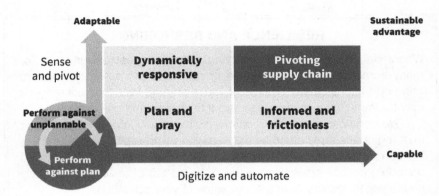

**Figure 1.3**   Sense and pivot
*Source:* Kearney analysis.

Indeed, Kearney does a great deal of work these days with our Resilience Stress Test, a customized study of a company's performance on selected resilience indicators across eight dimensions, such as geography, suppliers, and outbound logistics.[5] Companies use the test as a tool to focus, prioritize, and accelerate their resilience-building efforts. They look across five performance dimensions: cost, cash, service, resilience, and sustainability. We encourage them to identify and work on their weak spots, such as inadequate planning processes, overreliance on select overseas geographies, or lack of product platform and manufacturing flexibility.[6] Sometimes that involves reshoring (see the sidebar, "Resilience and Reshoring").

People sometimes think of *pivot* only in terms of suppliers: pivoting from one supplier to another. But the ability to pivot is valuable in responding to all types of risks throughout the value chain. For example, when Warby Parker encouraged online customers to order multiple designs of the same eyeglasses, returning the ones they didn't like, it was enhancing its ability to pivot on the customer dimension. Likewise, a pharmaceutical company might invest in seamless omnichannel distribution to pivot in the face of advances or disruptions in logistics.[8]

This book is a strategic tour of these principles. Although this format doesn't permit us to individualize the analysis to your specific

## RESILIENCE AND RESHORING

Where do *reshoring* and *nearshoring* fit into resilient operations? For many companies, the emergence of risks has prompted a desire to bring operations closer to home. If you're starting from that instinct, you may be impatient with our ideas about resilience and pivoting.

We certainly agree that reshoring is extremely important. You can't trust a global supply chain as much as the world previously thought. In the current global situation, dependencies on distant geographies and uncertain politics are a huge issue. Your pursuit of resilience will likely cause you to reshore or nearshore some of your operations.[7]

But which operations? You can't reshore everything. You have to think through the risks and benefits. When we say that the previous paradigm was *too* focused on reducing costs, we're not saying that costs are irrelevant. We're saying that you need to balance costs against other factors. And we believe the best way to summarize those factors is operations resilience.

For example, a 10% cost savings looks good for the procurement department. But if you achieve it at the risk of losing 10% of your sales due to disruptions and supply shortages, it may not be worthwhile. Of course, those risks are hard to quantify. But it seems quite clear that they are increasing. At minimum, you certainly need to analyze them. That's what the resilience lens can do for you.

Thus, each of the principles in this book may contribute to a reshoring/nearshoring decision. Working through the principles could help you decide to change the location of a certain function because it provides you with more resilience against supply shocks, or against demand shocks, or both. Reshoring could help you build better teams, improve technology, enhance sustainability, or all or none of these options. The point is that rather than starting from a desire to reshore, you can start from a framework that helps you make these *and other* decisions. Because the point isn't reshoring for its own sake. The point is reshoring in support of resilient operations.

situation, we can share with you what we've learned. We believe the message is clear: you must make your operations more resilient—and you *can* make your operations more resilient. This is how you build advantage.

## Insights Become Principles

Mastering operations resilience is clearly possible. Tools to address it include a holistic risk operating model, software packages and AI solutions, a commitment to transparency, and old-fashioned human ingenuity. But mastery doesn't happen on its own. It happens only when a company's leadership gives attention, focus, and talent to operational challenges.

Which challenges? We looked across operations to identify the areas with the most promise of return on investment. You could think of them as the fundamentals of resilient operations, or the areas of particular disruption, or the initiatives where we have noticed firms making particular progress. They can be summarized as supply chain, customers, employees, technology, and sustainability. Of course, there's overlap among them. And, of course, not every fundamental applies in every situation. Our purpose here is to lay out a philosophy of interacting with the VUCA world. As you design your own corporate strategy, you will pick, choose, and combine among these areas.

We distilled our insights in these areas into five business principles. They're not new (nor should they be). Instead their value comes from applying them to the risky business situations that require resilience.

Here are the five principles (see Figure 1.4):

1. Build resilience against supply shocks by empowering your supply base
2. Build resilience against demand shocks by using your operations to create customer value
3. Create resilient teams by leaning into new ways of working and the benefits of diversity
4. Enable resilience through technology by combining human judgment with artificial intelligence
5. Ensure long-term resilience by embracing sustainability

We'll discuss each in more detail in subsequent chapters. And we'll include examples of companies embracing resilience. Each example centers on a *leading* principle, but it also shows how the principles often

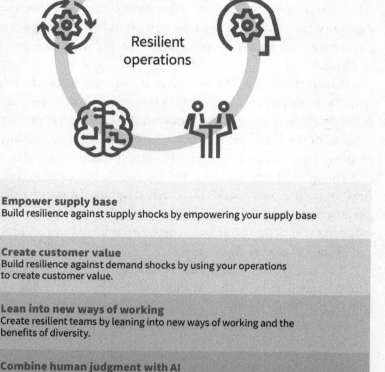

Figure 1.4    Five principles for resilient operations
*Source:* Kearney analysis.

combine. Because—let's reemphasize—this is a journey. You won't just issue an edict encouraging the firm to focus on operations. And you won't abandon your previous strengths, be they unique products or structural cost advantages or powerful relationships. Instead, similar to a hero setting off on a quest, you will take these (and other, perhaps not yet realized) strengths to new lands. You will face surprising threats and seemingly impossible challenges. You may at times question your wisdom in setting out on the journey. You will almost surely end it with a different inner character than when you started. But if you do indeed navigate the challenges, you will be hugely successful.

Let's dive in!

CHAPTER 2

# Principle 1:
## Build Resilience Against Supply Shocks by Empowering Your Supply Base

### Vanishing Semiconductors Demonstrate Supply Chain Breakdowns

The story of semiconductors in automobiles may be the best example of how the pandemic revealed broken supply chains. Most people know the basics: when COVID-19 hit, demand for new cars came to a virtual standstill. To save money and protect workers, automakers closed factories and canceled orders. Their suppliers thus did the same, and so did their suppliers—all up to the foundries manufacturing the base silicon wafers needed for computer chips. After they closed, the foundries needed time to ramp back up their capacity. And as they did so, they focused on their highest-margin products. In particular, they saw increased demand for home appliances and expansion of 4G/5G networks. Then, when demand for new cars suddenly shot up in the fourth quarter of 2020, automakers couldn't find the semiconductors they needed. Nearly all automakers had to curtail production. New car inventories dropped by as much as 70%; with too little supply to meet demand, sales dropped by as much as 54%.[1]

The situation smacked all the weaknesses of lean manufacturing methods. Automakers reduced costs by reducing inventory; then they ran out of inventory. They squeezed suppliers for every last penny; then they found themselves squeezed. They pushed risks ever-farther upstream; then they found those risks had flowed everywhere downstream.

The fault lay with a system, not any individual company. One problem was that semiconductors were in everything: vehicle microcontrollers as well as door locks, sophisticated automatic transmissions as well as bun-warming seat heaters. Even automakers with many different tier 1 and tier 2 suppliers found that those suppliers depended on the same chip foundries upstream. Another problem was also that automakers preferred semiconductors of a 200 mm wafer size—an older design that was cost-effective and reliable—rather than graduating to the newer and superior 300 mm wafer. In other words, rigid technology specs made for dependence on an obsolete product that was a low priority for foundries. But complicated engineering made it hard for automakers to switch. A third problem was a complex and geographically dispersed supply chain. Many semiconductors make the equivalent of three full trips around the world, crossing international borders 70 or more times in the manufacturing process.

One reason automakers had thrived in the previous outsourcing era was that they had a great deal of power over suppliers. But as automobile design became more complex, more digitized, and more semiconductor-dependent, the power dynamics reversed. The Tesla Model 3, for example, has 3.5 times the semiconductor elements as an average 2017 car (although Tesla, starting its engineering from scratch, was able to avoid some of the crisis). At the same time, demand for semiconductors—often 200 mm wafers—also exploded from non-automotive industries, such as companies making equipment to work with the Internet of Things. Then the foundries faced what were coming to be seen as "normal" supply chain issues: US-China political tensions, logistical disruptions, a blizzard in Texas, a factory fire in Japan, and the Ukraine war constricting the supply of a neon gas essential to the manufacturing process.

Automakers, with their deliberately downsized storage capacities and short order lead times, were only able to respond to a limited extent. They were largely dependent on the actions of their suppliers, to whom they had transferred the risks and responsibility for supply chain. Worse, some automakers lacked transparency. They found out too late that their tier 1 suppliers could not deliver the products that their assembly lines needed.[2]

But it's important not to blame automakers, because the problem wasn't theirs—or at least not theirs alone. The problem was a system that left all decision-makers with few good options in a crisis. And the crisis isn't just *pandemic*. The problem is that such a brittle system can be overwhelmed by crises big or small, medical or geopolitical, related to semiconductors or any other tiny but essential input.

This is lack of resilience. A company struggles to respond to the crisis of the pandemic, and then struggles to respond to an unexpected surge in demand, and then struggles to respond to the ongoing crises that seem par for the course these days. One way to build resilience against the next supply shock is to restructure your brittle supply chains so that they bend instead of breaking. So that the pressures are distributed across the network instead of concentrated at single-source dependencies.

One automaker bucked trends, delaying impacts from the semiconductor crisis: Toyota. You may find that surprising, given that Toyota is so closely associated with lean manufacturing and just-in-time inventory management. But after the 2011 Tohoku earthquake, Toyota doubled the value of inventory it carried. Its rich communication with suppliers led it to keep up to four months of stock for crucial components such as semiconductors. Its oft-misunderstood interpretation of lean manufacturing is not so much about reducing costs as it is paying attention to its supply chains. Part of that attention included working to identify and minimize risks. Toyota didn't avoid the crisis. Shortages extended so long that it eventually felt impacts along with everyone else. But its initial response showed more resilience than many competitors.[3]

As Toyota's example shows, to deal with disruptions, you need to lean into resilience. Yet because disruptions are so varied, you need not just scraps of resilient behavior, but a philosophy of resilience that guides all of your operations. Rather than squeezing profits out of a rigid, low-cost supply chain, companies need to empower an integrated ecosystem of collaborative suppliers.

## Empowered Suppliers Build Resilience

To improve resilience, you can start by changing your view of suppliers. They are a *source of value*. Rather than seeing your supply chain as something *you* construct out of meaningless individual chain links, envision your suppliers as partners. They need to be strong, because without them, you can't build a strong supply chain.

*Sure,* you may be thinking, *you're talking about supplier relationship management (SRM).* Yes and no. You do need relationships with your suppliers. And those relationships will be stronger when you manage them. But some people seem to think that SRM is all about bashing vendors over the head until they reduce the price another 4%. That's not a relationship. Those people are practicing supplier abuse management. As in any relationship, SRM involves communication on the executive level to understand the problems of the other party.

For example, Rational, a company that makes equipment for professional kitchens, won the 2022 Overall category for Kearney's Factory of the Year program by working in very close collaboration with suppliers. Rational's SRM focuses on technologies, quality criteria, and building long-term trust so that suppliers are willing to make mutually beneficial investments. Rational's supplier fitness programs are about managing growth together. For example, if Rational needs suppliers to commit to higher volumes, it sends experts to help implement and optimize, to ensure that development is sustainable for all parties.

Do your suppliers help you with design? Are they involved in open collaboration, with teams at your company, or teams at your other suppliers? Have you given them the visibility they need to make smart and profitable decisions? When you ask these types of questions, you know you're in a relationship. It's managing these issues—collaboration, transparency, satisfaction—that's the heart of your SRM.[4] Why? Because your suppliers are a source of value, and you need to maximize that value, not minimize the cost.

We're not saying, "Don't pay attention to costs." Just, "Don't pay attention *only* to costs." For example, when a global food business decided to reduce packaging costs, it shared detailed cost and complexity models with its packaging suppliers. That sparked collaborative ideation that not only further reduced costs but also improved packaging sustainability.

Indeed, for key suppliers, they should be more than *sources of value*. They should be *partners*. You are on a journey to resilience, and you want one or more suppliers to join you on this journey. This requires a new mindset. Rather than being transactional, your relationship with this supplier is one of *trust*. You trust them, they trust you. The top leadership of your firm invests the time and money required to build up that trust. Trust is always a two-way street:

- You may help suppliers in their time of need, trusting that they will help you come your own crises.
- They may ask to see your sales and operations planning (S&OP) details, trusting that you will fix anything that's wrong. After all, if you have S&OP issues, your suppliers often pay the price—but lack the power to fix them.
- You may ask to see your supplier's books, knowing that they will trust you not to negotiate on cost. Instead you want to see where they are struggling and how a joint effort might allay that struggle. For example, if they're struggling with their own suppliers, you may be able to help with negotiations or reengineering.

You certainly can't do this with *all* suppliers. Your engineers are going to travel to their site, your chief procurement officer (CPO) is going to meet with their CEO, and even your CEO will ideally meet their CEO. Obviously, this is only for major suppliers of huge quantities on multimillion dollar contracts. The benefit of bringing in the CPO or CEO, rather than a category manager, is that you may be able to get a longer-term contract. Yet even as you build this trust with major suppliers, you can let that new attitude spill over to other relationships. You can seek to establish a cooperative culture toward suppliers in general—note that it's the job of the C-suite to cultivate this culture.

Resilience is about strengthening the links in your chain. Building trust with key suppliers provides the strength. Thus empowering suppliers builds resilience. When they're resilient, the next crisis won't break them. It won't tempt them to move to other customers. And thus it won't break you.

## End-to-End Thinking Builds Resilience

Supplier partnerships are not just about shared spreadsheets and engineering specs. They're also about story. Your suppliers should be able to see an end-to-end picture: how their inputs bring value to the final product. For example, if you make automobiles and your steel producer understands your technical specs, that's good. But if the producer also understands that your customer is looking for a cool design, that's a partnership. That's a producer who will potentially contribute to your next cool design.

Likewise, if you make iPhones, your supplier should understand more than the value of Apple. (*"Ooh, Apple is a powerful company, I'd better do exactly as they say."*) Instead your supplier should understand the customer's value: the value of having glass that I can touch, but that doesn't break if I drop it. That's a supplier who builds your priorities into its decisions. (*"Ooh, my engineers just stumbled across a way to make that glass thinner. Let me tell Apple!"*)

But how is the supplier going to gain that knowledge? From your procurement team. These people used to do what we call "desktop procurement"—research into markets, costs, prices, and so on. Instead, they need to get to know suppliers and their products. Specifically, your procurement teams need *knowledge of how suppliers create value for us* and *knowledge of how we create value for customers.* The more they know about each, the more they can collaborate, develop, reengineer, and otherwise transform the supply chain. Indeed, when you have great answers to both questions, you become a disruptor—someone who can overcome industry thinking in a radical way.[5]

In other words, your category buyers need to be real *managers* of the category. If they just focus on "How can I get savings?" they do not have the big picture. They need to know everything about the market: What are the technologies? What is unique? What is distinctive about each supplier? We'll get into the implementation details in Chapter 8, but this is why they matter. And this is why the right goals and incentives must be in place.

For example, when a manufacturer of industrial assets had an opportunity to switch cable suppliers, the category manager did more than look at the 25% savings opportunity. She called engineering to learn how the cables were used, what drove materials costs, and what drove total cost of ownership. She learned that cheaper cables might break on average within four years rather than five—but the product had a five-year warranty. The company would be more resilient by rejecting the switch and discussing collaborative cost reductions with the incumbent supplier. But would she have made that choice if her incentives measured only procurement savings?

Yet supplier management is not merely a job for procurement. Your entire firm must think end-to-end about resilient supply chains. For example, if procurement is going to find alternative materials, it needs support from R&D. And if it's going to qualify those materials, it needs testing support from manufacturing.

Furthermore, a resilient supply chain may require devolved and decentralized decision-making to manage the inevitable disruptions. If a tree falls across a remote shipping lane and no *Wall Street Journal* reporter is there to hear it, does it have an impact? Most decidedly yes—and the news will reach your local representatives long before it reaches those involved in top-down decision-making.

Indeed, modern supply networks have become so complex that no single player within them has the power to control the whole value chain from material extraction through to consumption. You can no longer use the traditional siloed approach to managing them. Everyone needs to collaborate more. All participants—from sub-tier suppliers to tech platforms, producers, and distributors—need to deploy predictive data analytics to achieve maximum visibility. You want visibility into changing demand and supply constraints as they emerge, as well as visibility into hidden risks that could be lurking both upstream and downstream.[6]

This is why we talk about supplier *ecosystems* and *empowering* those ecosystems. The phrase *supply chain* is still handy because so many people know what it means. But in a sense both parts of it are outdated: (1) you're no longer looking at supplies that arrive at your factory; instead, you're looking at a value chain that goes all the way to the end consumer. (2) It shouldn't be a *chain*, with all the *weakest-link* implications of that word; instead, you should lean into the interdependencies and manage it as an ecosystem.

## Reshoring Builds Resilience

Given that reshoring is such a hot topic, some of you may be wondering why this chapter hasn't addressed it yet. The answer is that we think reshoring is great. It can reduce risk and create value. About 40% of companies we work with have either already moved some of their sourcing and manufacturing closer to home markets or plan to do so within the next three years. But it does come with costs. You can't reshore everything. So as you think about *what* to reshore, you need this broader resilience mindset. Where does reshoring fit into your supplier ecosystem and end-to-end thinking?

To summarize the trade-off: reshoring (or nearshoring or "friend-shoring," when you use suppliers in countries with shared values) offers logistical, strategic, and brand image advantages. However, you're going to pay more for labor, and it'll be hard to find both labor and deep manufacturing expertise. You won't necessarily reduce your carbon footprint—you'll save on transportation, but developing a second source closer to home might mean adding another factory to the world. Technology can help, as we'll discuss in Chapter 5. But even that technology requires investments—where should you invest first?

Answer: with your newer, higher-margin products. Higher-margin products (such as medical devices) are often more complex. That means they can benefit from the new technologies that you will likely deploy during reshoring. The higher margins mean that you face higher risks from disruptions in far-flung supply chains. And when you consider the total amount of margin repatriated (instead of total cost savings), the business case for reshoring becomes compelling.[7]

With reshoring, you're often seeking to address risks associated with geographically dispersed supply chains. You may want to explicitly set that objective: to move to multiple *multi-local* supply chains. They're still connected via a global governance function, but you're making things *in the market, for the market.* Some companies may seek regional self-sufficiency: Europe, for example, could be a bubble of interconnected supply and demand nodes. Other companies may maintain existing supply chains while complementing them with new, scalable production bases closer to the target customer markets. And some companies will use both approaches ambidextrously—a multi-local approach for the inputs that most drive value and single global supply chain for high-volume inputs.

But there has to be something new and different about your newly reshored facilities: benefits from automation, or state-of-the-art production innovations, or reduced cycle times, or proximity to customers. If you just replicate what you have in a low-cost country at a location closer to home, you're not creating resilience. You're just increasing costs.

These strategic considerations will vary by industry (see Figure 2.1). It matters how complex your current supply chain is and how asset-intensive it is. It matters where your components or critical raw materials come from. Do you have automated factories that depend on high utilization? If so—for example, in high tech and semiconductors—it will be harder to establish redundancies. Have existing suppliers clustered geographically? If so—for example, in automotive—it will be harder to move assembly plants away from the parts they assemble. Is your industry highly regulated? If so—for example, in pharmaceuticals—it will be harder and more time-consuming to move production and obtain requisite licensing and permits. Your reshoring decisions should be tied to the (re-)design of your end-to-end network.[8]

When we say that you need to embrace end-to-end thinking, we mean that you should move from a traditional *rigid and siloed* supply chain model to one that may be described as *unchained.* It's unchained because you reduce or eliminate boundaries. You add agility (often through technology, as we'll discuss in Chapter 5). With this flexibility, you create supply chains that can not only survive inevitable disruptions but also actually learn from them and come back both smarter and stronger (see the sidebar, "Case Example: Strengthening the Supply Base Through Strategic Collaborations and Reshoring").[9] That's resilience.

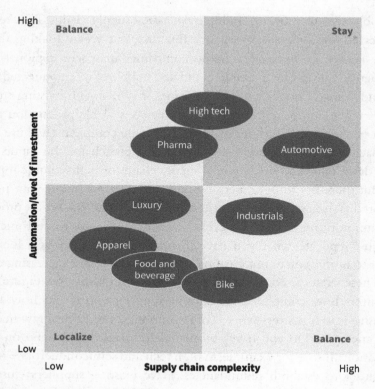

**Figure 2.1**   Choices about reshoring

*Source:* Kearney analysis.

## CASE EXAMPLE: STRENGTHENING THE SUPPLY BASE THROUGH STRATEGIC COLLABORATIONS AND RESHORING

An industrial company had dozens of factories around the world. Many of its inputs were single-sourced, and it had high exposure to Southeast Asia. It became worried about the volatility of its supply market. It was concerned about potential risks such as COVID-19, geopolitical tensions, and natural disasters—as well as sustainability, ethical sourcing, and traceability of inputs.

It started by mapping its spend. It developed a complex database about even its most obscure parts and materials providers. What company makes the surface treatments that go on a particular subassembly? And where is it located? What company makes the lubricant used on the adjacent rubber pieces? Does the subassembly use any end-of-life components that would soon go out of production? The company wanted to know. That way it could identify hot spots.

Because the mapping effort involved tier 2 and even tier 3 suppliers, the company had to work closely with its tier 1 suppliers. How else could it know about potential supply shocks? If just one sub-component became unavailable, the company wouldn't be able to make its final products. Yet in many cases, finding an alternative tier 1 supplier wouldn't necessarily solve the problem, because everybody depended on availability of the same tier 2 components. To ensure healthy collaboration, the company built trust with long-term tier 1 suppliers. For example, it shared its business direction and priorities, and asked the supplier what internal changes it needed to make to improve the supplier's efficiency.

For simple products, the company could diversify its portfolio. It made sure to maintain production processes in at least two relevant regions. It engaged in strategic and systematic double sourcing across its supply chain. It planned ahead to improve recovery from unexpected disruptions. It developed an early-warning system for shortages. It identified a subset of inputs that simply needed stockpiling.

For some inputs, it was harder to find a viable second source. So the company sought to learn more and deepen its relationships with those suppliers. A few were in trouble. For example, one was facing increasing costs of labor and materials to the point where it might soon become insolvent. So the company started a supplier fitness program.

- In a first step, it improved the supplier's credit rating by giving a letter of intent and guarantees to the supplier's bank.
- In a second step, it supported ad-hoc negotiations with the supplier's suppliers. The negotiations focused on reducing cost increases as much as possible.
- In a third step, the two companies jointly explored material and process levers to further reduce costs. For example, some situations provided opportunities to switch to a different material. In other cases, they could streamline the manufacturing process.

*(continued)*

*(continued)*

Conversations at the C-level of both firms ensured trust and alignment on both sides. The industrial company made sure to understand the supplier's capacity, capability, and performance to avoid placing orders that would put undue pressure on its principles—that would cause it to cut corners or abuse employees or pollute the environment.

Some of the company's suppliers were both critical and successful, but they were subject to risks such as geopolitical instability and complicated logistics. The company worked with these suppliers to diversify geographically. Could they collaborate to develop a second source closer to the manufacturing operations? They didn't necessarily call this *reshoring*, because these hubs were still globally dispersed. And, indeed, the more-local sources couldn't cover 100% of an adjacent factory's volume. But they could cover 20–30% of that volume—and there were opportunities to scale up. This effort was by far the most complex and challenging component of the company's strategy, and it is still in process. But the company has confidence in success due to its transparency and strong collaborations with its supply base.

CHAPTER 3

# Principle 2:
## Build Resilience Against Demand Shocks by Using Your Operations to Create Customer Value

### Lessons from Fast Fashion

Any industry is fascinating to those inside of it. But sometimes an industry is fascinating for being the first to transform—in a transformation that will soon hit other industries.

From 2002 to 2017, the global apparel industry had a compound annual growth rate of 8%. Global textile revenues grew from about $1 trillion in 2002 to almost $3 trillion in 2015. And during that time, the number of garments purchased annually grew by 60%.[1] You could view this development as a triumph of globalization: companies could make clothing more cheaply, and people everywhere had more money to spend on it. In the same way that Henry Ford made cars that his employees could afford, the global fashion industry cut costs to expand its audience. (There's also a dark underbelly to this story in the form of horrific performance on environmental, social, and governance (ESG) issues, which we will address in Chapter 6.)

But this was not a traditional *lean* success story. In fact, what drove the explosive growth was a revolution in how to *create value for the customer*. Obviously all apparel brands have always been customer-focused, because you need to make clothing that people want to wear. But traditionally, that development cycle happened in a fairly rigid 24-month timeline. A fashion designer—an artist—would create a look. It would be revealed in an haute couture world of runway shows and breathless press coverage. Then would follow months of anticipation as these soon-to-trend fashions moved from *high end* to *high street*—from the cloistered world of fashionistas to the profitable world of retail, from design to operations, from idea to profit.

*Fast fashion* disrupted all of that. Companies such as Zara, H&M, Topshop, and Primark centered their operations on the customer rather than the designer. Early in the revolution, when a fashion week extravaganza revealed customers' desires for a certain look, fast-fashion brands made sure that their operations could quickly and cheaply produce something close to that look. Their efficient operations delivered on customers' desires faster than the old model.

Then these brands started releasing new products continuously, rather than in defined seasons. Zara might offer hundreds of new items a week, in very small quantities. This turned out to be a perfect match with fashion consumers, who are among the most fickle consumers in the world. They enjoyed shopping frequently. They were motivated by the sense of scarcity, the idea that these limited-quantity items might not be available next week. They felt little obligation to the formalities and schedules of the high-fashion gurus. Their tastes would change overnight.

Everyone knew this about consumers. Everyone knew that product life cycles were necessarily short. So why did traditional brands commit to long cycles of product development and manufacturing? They had valid historical reasons: it was hard to know which fashions people would turn to next, which increased dependence on the haute couture world; mass marketing could extend product life cycles, when consumers all watched the same network television shows; primitive technology made few other options available. But the fast-fashion disrupters saw—before their competitors did—that changing conditions could give them competitive advantage.

Thus even at the height of the lean, globalized supply chain—in the 1990s and early 2000s—these disrupters shifted to a quick-response supply chain. For example, Zara invested in capital-intensive operations, such as computer-guided fabric cutting, and kept this key differentiator in-house rather than outsourcing it. Zara did outsource sewing and other labor-intensive operations, but to seamstresses near its headquarters in Galicia, Spain. Seamstresses in Asia would have been cheaper. But longer transport times were too high a price to pay—because Zara's priority was to operate *for the customer*, and its customers wanted fashion fast.[2]

It's one thing to start a revolution. It's another to begin a transformation journey that keeps you on the cusp of subsequent revolutions. Since the early 2000s, new innovations have enabled brands to get even closer to consumers and use those insights to change their operations. For example, you might bypass physical retail to sell directly from websites. You might introduce thousands rather than hundreds of new items every week. You might start taking signals from social media influencers instead of fashion week bloggers. And you might shift your marketing to those influencers rather than glossy magazines. Such trends are sometimes summarized as *ultra-fast fashion*.

These innovations have, in turn, resulted in new opportunities. For example, when you focus on micro-influencers rather than fashion week runway models, you discover opportunities in plus-size or other niches. When your strength is a quick-response supply chain rather than a lowest-cost one, you gain resilience against sudden changes in styles. And when you move away from reliance on physical retail, you gain resilience against a pandemic that shuts down all those stores.

Some analysts predicted that the pandemic would mark the end of fast fashion. Indeed, brands such as Primark were stranded with billions of dollars of inventory that couldn't be sold. However, online-only upstart Boohoo.com thrived. After all, the pandemic merely shifted *where* people bought clothes (from stores to websites) and *how* they showed them off (from parties to Instagram)—not their desire to be fashionable. Now customers wanted quarantine-themed fashions such as hoodies and sweatpants. The ultra-fast upstarts—even more dedicated to operating for the customer than their fast-fashion predecessors—had the quick-response value chains that could profitably serve them.[3]

One of the big lessons of fast fashion, then, is to structure your operations around customer needs. Not lowest costs, not traditional ways of doing business, not even the demands of your most talented artist/ designers. It's a lesson that's both intuitively obvious and very hard to implement. But buried inside it is another, even more obvious, even more difficult lesson. You don't just do it once. You don't implement a model of fast fashion in a physical retail environment, and commit to it forever. Instead you commit to always operating for the customer— always transforming.

Because make no doubt: fast fashion–style revolutions are coming for every industry. Maybe your customers aren't quite as fickle as fashion consumers. But they're fickle. After all, they're human. "The heart wants what it wants," as Emily Dickinson wrote. Your sales and marketing teams know this; they work hard to get as close to your customers' hearts as possible. Are you ready to constantly transform your operations to keep up?

## Know What Drives Customer Value

All companies like to believe that they are close to their customers, they understand their customers, and they operate for their customers. But how can you confirm this? Here's one great test: if customer preferences suddenly change, how quickly can that ripple through your operations? This is a measure of your resilience.

For example, imagine that you make bicycles. What color should they be? If you sell to wholesalers, who sell to retailers, who own the customer relationships, you may struggle to answer that question. You could ask fashion gurus what colors are generally popular this year, but you're not actually operating for your customers, because you're not talking to them. This is the appeal of direct-to-consumer sales channels: it's not just the money you save by cutting out the intermediary, it's the customer intimacy you gain.[4]

Even if you have customer intimacy, however, two problems remain. First, are you asking your customers the right questions, collecting the right data, and then actually using it? If you always ask the same customers, or always immediately after buying the bicycle, you may not really understand bicycle customers. You understand only a subset of customers who happen to use these outlets, and you understand only their purchasing decision, not their bicycling habits. (And you may not even understand that if the data just sits on a server getting dusty.) Second—and most relevant to our purposes here—do you have the capabilities to alter your operations accordingly? If you learn that customers want yellow bicycles, can you make them? Operational flexibility gives you resilience against changing customer needs.

When it comes to new products, the keyword is *design-to-value* (DtV). We believe that your DtV approach should be elevated, agile, and crowdsourced. Elevated: CXO-sponsored and jointly led by the chief marketing officer and chief supply chain officer. Agile: deployed via an agile process in which innovative and imperfect ideas are promptly tested with suppliers and consumers. Crowdsourced: involving procurement, supply chain leaders, outside product and package design experts, technical services, and customer sentiment analysts from day one. Compared to a point solution, this DtV approach better addresses the interlocking challenges of cost, supply/demand uncertainty, and sustainability.[5]

By the way, hidden in our bicycle example for this section is an assumption worth questioning. What if your customers don't much care what color their bicycle is?

## Drive Out Complexity

Complexity can be both expensive and fragile. When you have lots of different products, in lots of sizes or assortments or flavor combinations, your operational challenges drive up costs and increase risks. You may thus be hesitant to solicit customer opinion, because it would only further increase complexity.

But consumers, too, often hate complexity. And retailers also hate complexity: knowing that more stock-keeping units (SKUs) lead to more out-of-stocks, they're always pursuing SKU optimization. So you can use a customer lens to redesign your product portfolios for simplicity. And as you do so, you can design them for operational ease, modularity, and resilience.[6]

One great example is LEGO, the world's biggest and most profitable toy maker. Our colleagues built two of its 3,600-piece models: the Lamborghini Sián FKP 37 and Bugatti Chiron. They found that these two models share 75% of brick designs (not accounting for color) with just 6% and 12% of the bricks being unique to those sets respectively.

What LEGO is doing is applying *platform* principles to its product design. A platform is a shared set of common design, engineering, and operational practices, and shared components, across a set of outwardly distinct products. Platforming sustainably supports variety where it matters—to the customer—while minimizing operational complexity on the back end. Product design platforms enable you to customize a wide range of items by drawing from a shared set of thoughtfully crafted modules. With platforming, you can minimize the risks of demand variability because you have fungible building blocks that can quickly be configured into any number of end products.

For example, the mattress company Helix Sleep asks customers to take a quiz to determine their unique requirements: firmness, motion transfer, temperature regulation, and so on. Does Helix Sleep then custom-design and build a mattress to those exact specs? No. Instead, it draws from fewer than a dozen preconfigured mattress constructions to satisfy the vast majority of outcomes from the user preference quiz.[7]

However, note that genuine resilience requires more than slapping a customer survey on the front end of a traditional portfolio optimization project. Why? Because you're not just simplifying SKUs. You're simplifying supply chains, processes, tech stacks, and IT systems. Too often, portfolio simplification initiatives hide rather than eliminate complexity, especially on the back end.

Instead, you should see portfolio simplification as part of a broader transformation toward resilience. It starts with getting closer to the customer, identifying what drives customer value. It continues through reducing both the Q (quantities of SKUs) and the P (processes and systems supporting those SKUs). It welcomes the cross-functional implications of those efforts (see Figure 3.1). Indeed, it may even seek to broaden those implications across the entire supply chain.[8]

## Creative Customer Listening

The pandemic messed with traditional retail calendars. The 2020 back-to-school sales happened when few parents knew for sure if their kids would even go back to a physical school. Black Friday sales happened when customers were still supposed to be always keeping six feet apart.

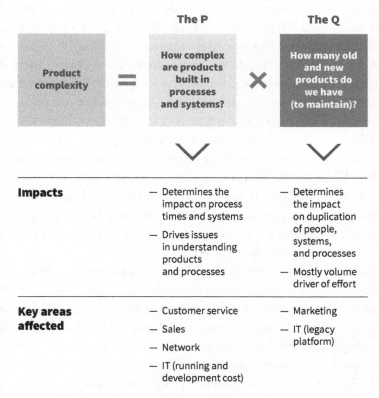

**Figure 3.1**   Reducing portfolio complexity
*Source:* Kearney analysis.

But we think the disruptions didn't go far enough. Wouldn't it be better if swimsuits were actually available in July? If Christmas merchandise didn't show up before Halloween? If bedding went on sale before holiday visitors arrived, rather than in January?

In short, we propose that blind devotion to undifferentiated treadmill-like calendars isn't really consumer-centric. There's an opportunity to get closer to *your actual customers* by stepping away from "the way we've always done it." That's true not only for retailers and consumer packaged goods (CPG) companies, but for any company. Those capable of rewriting the rules of assortment, allocation, pricing, promotion, and fulfillment will be better able to adapt to whatever the future holds.[9]

However, getting there will take radical acts of listening. Sometimes that means actually connecting with customers, rather than letting their voices be filtered by retailers or wholesalers or their own subsequent reinterpretations. For example, the Kearney Consumer Institute (KCI) found that companies have to take care when talking to customers about quality and convenience, because those words can have different meanings at different points in the customer journey. For example, when surveyed about quality, consumers responded differently from when they were asked why they bought the product: highlighting *crunchy* for chips, rather than *craving*, and *durability and longevity* for small appliances, rather than *brand*.[10] Similarly, KCI found that consumers value *convenience,* but don't necessarily define it the way companies expect them to.[11] All of which implies that you have to work at actually hearing and trusting their input. Even when it's conflicted, you can't just ignore it in favor of whatever is most convenient for you.

Sometimes—especially in product development—big data can help. For example, a leading global fast-moving consumer goods (FMCG) company is continually adjusting to the needs of Chinese consumers, especially in the growing e-commerce channel. As it does so, it calls on partnerships with large platforms to capture consumer data. Its China-based digital innovation center links listening to customers (digital marketing, big data, artificial intelligence [AI]) with making its supply chains more efficient and intelligent. For Chinese markets, the company transformed its traditional stage-gate innovation process to reduce innovation cycles from the classic two years to about six months. It increased the success rate of new product launches by 60%. Meanwhile, it also was able to reduce inventory by 30% and reduce logistics costs by 15% while achieving 99.9% on-time delivery.

That's just one example of centering your operations on the customers. The company understood that Chinese customers could be different from other global customers, and that this was a form of demand variability that required resilience. So it invested in creative new ways of listening to customers—and made sure that its operations could respond.

## Navigate Demand to Improve the Supply Chain

So far in this chapter, we've talked about how knowledge of your customers' needs can help you adjust products, portfolios, and processes to strengthen your supply chain and become more resilient. But one can also shine the light in the other direction. You can achieve resilience by shaping demand.

It's funny how many companies overlook *supply chain planning* when they seek to improve operations. (Or, worse, they equate supply chain planning with a time-consuming overhaul of everything from forecasting accuracy to inventory management.) Sure, planning is difficult amid ongoing crises. But it's not useless. A grounded, bottom-up, tactical-first approach can help you manage inventory and maintain service levels. Furthermore, it can help you pinpoint the root causes of deeper supply chain issues. With conscious acts of planning, you can identify priority actions that generate quick, meaningful returns. For example, a personal care products company segmented its large portfolio by volume and volatility. Its high-volatility, high-volume items generated 43% of its revenues—this was where to focus actions such as beefing up safety stocks and seasonal inventories. By contrast, for more stable high-volume products, more value would come from honing the accuracy of the demand forecast.[12]

Such supply chain planning depends on forecasting and demand planning. Obviously demand can be unpredictable, especially in certain industries. But there are ways to sense, shape, and forecast it, especially with today's data analytics. For example, when you develop a *shape of demand* capability, you don't try to predict a future outcome 10 years in advance. Instead, you create scenarios and watch for inflection points that will determine supply chain investments.[13]

A full demand intelligence capability will guide your strategic decisions on merchandising, e-commerce, and your supply chain. It should offer predictive algorithms to forecast near- and long-term shape of demand; granular, geo-specific insights about demand; and nuanced understanding of demand drivers. The better you can understand your demand and what drives it, the more levers you have available to provide agility in a crisis.[14]

## Supply Chains Are Now Value Chains (If They Weren't Already)

*Supply chain* once referred to getting parts to the factory. But you must also get products from the factory to the consumer. With the rise of e-commerce, options to do so have proliferated—and highlighted new potential breaks in the chain, new needs for resilience. As you navigate these issues, it helps to have a North Star: always be creating value for the customer.

For example, take reshoring. Can reshoring help you create value for your customers? It's easy to imagine how—faster time to delivery is the most obvious answer, although your particular situation may suggest others. But your answer need not be generic. Do customers for *this specific product* value faster time to delivery? If not, then the product may not be a good candidate for reshoring. (If you don't know, then maybe investments in getting closer to your customers would be more valuable than investments in reshoring.)

Another much-talked about example is *last-mile delivery*. (It's now sometimes called *last-mile/first-mile*, to account for reverse logistics for returns.) When pandemic-fueled spikes in e-commerce led to shortages in delivery capacity, and thus skyrocketing prices, many companies responded with segmentation. For which customers was faster time to delivery both valued and possible? Those were the needs to be met.

The companies with less knowledge about what their consumers valued were at a disadvantage.[15]

More broadly, these examples point to the widening of the consumer end of the value chain. Where once consumers always bought products in stores, now omnichannel strategies are essential—for retailers and also for many manufacturers. This brings operational challenges that are often hard to solve. But putting in the effort to solve them brings two benefits. First, you become better at creating value for your customers. Second, you build more resilient operations. (See the sidebar, "Case Example: Driving Customer Value Through Demand Sensing and Product Design.") That link—between customer value and resilience—extends all the way up and down your value chain.

---

### CASE EXAMPLE: DRIVING CUSTOMER VALUE THROUGH DEMAND SENSING AND PRODUCT DESIGN

A global, multi-brand company in the CPG industry wanted to improve margins, build resilience, and drive customer value. It sold all sorts of diverse products—including toiletries and cosmetics such as shampoos, perfumes, and makeup—through retailers (both physical and online), rather than through its own sales channels. It realized that it needed to better listen to the voice of the consumer.

It decided to start with online sales. The company sold a lot of products through Amazon.com, and used the Amazon Forecast service to predict future sales. The forecasts were clearly related to the A9 algorithm, which Amazon uses to determine the relevance and ranking of products in search results. A9 uses a proprietary combination of machine learning and AI to analyze a wide range of factors, including product details, customer reviews, sales data, and advertising information. But the company was concerned that Forecast and A9 couldn't sufficiently consider external factors. Could it better predict and respond to unexpected search spikes? Could it better link demand factors to its supply chain? Could it improve its A9 rankings and thus goose demand?

*(continued)*

(*continued*)

The company identified market-specific external datasets that could enrich the Amazon forecasts. Improving the sell-out forecast reduced chargebacks, which improved search rankings. Meanwhile, the company's analysts sifted through 65 potential drivers of demand and supply, including internal factors such as product availability, pricing, and promotions. They identified just five of the drivers as key to improving forecasting and purchase order fulfillment:

- **Sales history:** Understanding the sales performance of a product in the past—including its sales velocity and product reviews—provided insights into customer behavior and purchasing patterns. That helped predict future demand.
- **Availability:** The product's lead time to ship and in-stock rate determined whether it was available for customers to buy. Ensuring that products were readily available and could be shipped quickly would maintain customer satisfaction and loyalty.
- **Competitiveness:** The product's price, compared to other similar products, was also a critical driver of demand. Adjusting pricing and promotions could help it remain competitive in the market.
- **Product reviews:** Products with high-quality reviews and a high number of ratings were typically more relevant and ranked higher in Amazon's search results.
- **Market trends:** Identifying seasonal trends, Google search trends, and other market trends helped the company better anticipate changes in demand and adjust the supply chain accordingly.

The results were positive. But the project also showed the company that data was an imprecise proxy for the voice of the consumer. It decided to bring both online and traditional customers into the product design process. It performed a *conjoint analysis* to understand which features consumers valued. Without such an exercise, brand and price were all it had to go on. But in one example case, it discovered that consumers placed equal value on factors such as the way the item's packaging closed for reuse, the item's texture, and transparency about its ingredients. These were all elements under the company's control—formulations that could be tweaked going forward.

When it knew more about what customers wanted, the company could reduce complexity. No need to produce bottles that closed in five different ways or products with varying textures. It could focus on the features that would really drive value. Reducing complexity lowered costs, thus increasing margins. Reducing complexity also improved resilience. Simplified operations could more quickly respond to changes in customer demand or crises along the supply chain.

This project had positive results. And it has shown the company the promise of new frontiers of customer-centric transformation. First, to simplify product portfolios, the company is now investigating platform principles in product design. Second, to further improve customer satisfaction, it wants to collaborate with selected suppliers to improve the aspects of its products that customers are most willing to pay for. Third, to maintain and enrich its understanding of those customer value drivers, it's experimenting with creative new ways to listen and to ensure that the voice of the customer ripples across all departments.

# CHAPTER 4

# Principle 3:
# Create Resilient Teams by Leaning into New Ways of Working and the Benefits of Diversity

## *CEOs Thrive When Their Employees Do*

Worried about being seen, the CEO sneaks into a dusty shack on the bad side of town, under a sign reading "Tarot. Palm reading. Astrology." Inside, an ethereally dressed woman takes the executive's hand and stares into it. Amazingly, she immediately homes in on the executive's biggest issue. She says, "You're wondering if you're going to be fired."

It wouldn't happen this way, would it? We all want to believe that CEO tenure depends on more than pseudo-science and intuition. But why *do* CEOs get fired? Our colleague Alex Liu analyzed CEO departures from 200 companies over two five-year periods: from 2011 to 2016 and from 2016 to 2021 (see Figure 4.1). The total amount of transitions remained relatively stable at 150 and 155, respectively. But the number of involuntary departures increased from 41 to 52. Furthermore, the involuntary departures triggered by causes other than financial factors increased nearly fivefold.[1]

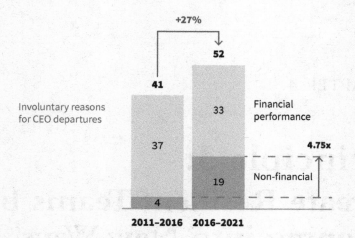

**Figure 4.1** Why CEOs get fired
*Sources:* ASX, Capital IQ, and Kearney analysis.

As Alex wrote, "This suggests that CEOs are becoming increasingly vulnerable to being removed from office for issues such as turning a blind eye to toxic corporate culture or failing to address socially irresponsible behavior among their employees." We'll put it more bluntly: it looks like CEOs are increasingly being fired for lousy team leadership rather than merely lousy financial results.

It shouldn't be surprising. The 2016–2021 period was full of cultural upheavals. Headlines included the #MeToo movement, the murder of George Floyd, and the January 6 attack on the US Capitol. But the biggest cultural change was the flavor of the response: a near-universal attitude of *Those people should lose their jobs.* Dismissals of insurrectionists, sexual abusers, and racists reflected a wider culture establishing a code of conduct. For example, a Central Park dog walker who filed a false police report against a Black birdwatcher in 2020 was fired from her insurance investment job the next day (and later lost her lawsuit of wrongful termination). Although she wasn't on company time and was charged with only a misdemeanor, her employer would not tolerate her racism. She lost her job because of reasons unrelated to financial performance. No wonder that's also happening to CEOs. As *Us Weekly* magazine might say, "CEOs: They're just like us."

But let's flip it around. CEOs can control their destiny. (Imagine that F. Scott Fitzgerald was reading *Us Weekly* and objected, "CEOs are different from you and me." Ernest Hemingway would have responded, "Yes; they have more workplace power.")[2] CEOs can thrive in their jobs by building a great workplace team and culture. Their boards will reward them not only for strong financial performance but also for creating a great place to work. Indeed, studies continually find that making employees happy is a great path to increasing shareholder value.[3]

That's especially true today. Because today you need a *resilient* workforce. You need people who are resilient in order to craft effective responses to a variety of crises. You need a collaborative sense of resilience to perform amid varying individual challenges. You need people who believe in resilience in order to foster it with suppliers, customers, technology, and sustainability. If people are your greatest asset, then collectively resilient people are your most resilient collective asset.

## People Build Resilience

Whatever your company does, resilience-wise, your people will do it. Your people will make the decisions, choose the technologies, talk to the suppliers, understand the customers, and develop the strategies. So you need people *skilled* in resilience—people who will choose resilient options instead of just cheap ones. You also need people to *be* resilient, to be calm and wise in a crisis. And you need resilient teams—because no individual is a superhero, but a team's collective talents can add up.

In other words, although we often think of resilience in terms of systems or organizations, it's also for people. Resilience requires certain skill sets. And that starts with hiring diverse. Of course this is the now-accepted lesson of diversity, equity, and inclusion (DEI) initiatives: diverse teams make better decisions. By seeing issues from multiple perspectives, they arrive at more resilient solutions. Note that under past conditions—when there was less volatility and fewer unexpected challenges—you weren't punished as much for a lack of diversity. Teams were always using the same skill sets. But today, when anything can happen, and fast, your teams need the more diverse perspectives to gain the more resilient solutions. Yet in order to staff diverse teams, you must first hire diverse people. *Diversity* here refers not only to diverse ethnicities, genders, and sexual orientations—which are indeed important—but also to diverse backgrounds, skills, and other characteristics.

Implementing workforce agility requires a shift in mindset that values people for their potential. You want to broaden your definition of an impressive résumé or CV. It's not just about replicating a team's existing skill sets or adding more Ivy Leaguers. Instead you complement your team with people who have unusual backgrounds. Two failed startups and a gap year abroad with an NGO may be the kind of life experience that demonstrates potential to deepen and expand skills. Then you commit to training in order to retain those talented folks. For example, an electronics manufacturing services company developed fit-for-purpose training opportunities for qualities such as instilling a quality-focused mindset; negotiation, communication, collaboration, and technical skills; and financial training. It was aligning on skills rather than traditional measures of success, such as where someone went to school or their tenure in a role.[4]

Thus, you may want to do your own gap analysis on your needed skills, and your needed perspectives. Then, in order to fill those gaps, you'll need to develop and sustain a winning employee value proposition (EVP). What do your employees truly value, and what do you offer to help them have the best experience on the job? For example, a retail chain facing more than 100% employee turnover in distribution centers evaluated its EVP, identified gaps, and developed short- and long-term measures to be competitive. Its insights included the fact that employees appreciated the company's culture and career development opportunities—but these could be better used in recruitment. Meanwhile, satisfaction with the compensation package differed by length of tenure, which suggested refined approaches to wage adjustments. The resulting changes cut turnover by more than half, dramatically increased productivity, and improved service levels in ways that led to increased customer satisfaction.[5]

Of course, it's not enough to hire for diversity and skills. You also have to productively manage those diverse teams. To unleash people's vast potential, you need to fuel their imagination and motivation. A new generation of passionate talents need guidance—and can offer support. Thus your leaders and middle managers may need coaching in, among other skills, how to conduct authentic dialogues. Employees today want their leaders to earn respect through authenticity and accountability. Authority alone is no longer enough—leaders need to trust their teams more and be their genuine selves. In short, they need to align on purpose and joy.[6]

## Purpose and Joy Build Resilience

The world faces a *purpose gap.* When it comes to corporate social responsibility (CSR) commitments, there's a gap between intention and action in delivering meaningful change. This matters for the future of human society, but it also matters for your employees' sense of fulfillment. Paul Polman, the former CEO of Unilever, observed that people "don't want to look back at what they've done and say, 'Well, I built market share of Dove 4.5 percent . . .' No, they want to say, 'I helped so many millions of women achieve self-esteem. I helped so many people improve their nutrition levels and, in doing so, I've actually strengthened the institution I represent.' And that is really purpose in action."[7]

What is your company's purpose? If you're going to be resilient, it has to be more than "creating value for shareholders." Yet ironically, by becoming a more purpose-driven organization, you may well create more value for shareholders. Purpose-activated companies benefit from greater customer loyalty and better employee performance and retention. They also outperform the stock market, grow faster than the average company, and report higher levels of innovation. Purpose is a powerful lever to create value.[8]

So you need a purpose statement. More than that, what you really need to do is *implement purpose in your operations.* Only 45% of companies have done so—that's the gap between purpose and action.[9] But here's the key point for this chapter: it's also the gap between the boardroom and average employees. CXOs score their companies about 40% higher on purpose metrics than middle managers. Among younger and entry-level survey respondents, the scores were even worse.[10]

In short, employees aren't feeling as fulfilled at work as bosses. Perhaps that explains the *joy gap*. Our colleague Alex Liu found that more than half of surveyed working adults felt less joy at work than they'd expect. The results held across all generations, geographies, and organizational levels. And it got worse in the pandemic (see Figure 4.2).[11]

We know how people experience joy at work: through harmony, acknowledgment, and impact. They want to feel aligned and united with their teams, and appreciated for their contributions. They also want to understand the purpose and power of their work.

The gaps are related. You can solve the joy gap by solving the purpose gap: by aligning people's personal purpose with the organization's purpose. You define your company's purpose in a way that people (not just CXOs) can relate to. Then you build your EVP based on that purpose. You also build formal and informal mechanisms to ensure that leaders and employees live that purpose.

Purpose should arise organically from emotions, rather than being manufactured. Employees "need to understand their own purpose, not a leader's narrative about purpose," Alex wrote. To do so, he said elsewhere, "Employees need to feel worthy of bringing their full and complete self

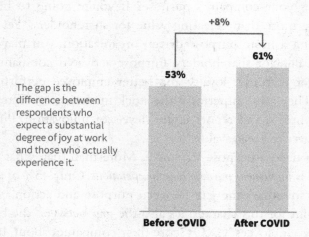

The gap is the difference between respondents who expect a substantial degree of joy at work and those who actually experience it.

+8%

53%    61%

**Before COVID**    **After COVID**

**Figure 4.2**  The joy gap at work
*Source:* Kearney analysis.

to work." They need to feel authentic.[12] Here is how purpose ties back to your DEI priorities. For decades, most companies refused to let their employees be authentic: to be queer, or Black, or female, or tattooed, or pregnant, or needing to work from home on Tuesdays, or uncomfortable in a white button-down shirt and dark tie. Seventy years ago, companies aligned their employees on such superficial issues of presentation. Now, companies can allow employees to align themselves on purpose.

Why should companies make this change? Because firms that succeed at instilling a culture of purpose in their employees will perform better in a volatile environment. The employees know why they are dealing with day-to-day challenges—not for a paycheck, but for a purpose. Thus they will push harder to overcome those challenges. They will be resilient.

## Economies of Skill Build Resilience

The old, cost-focused supply chains were built on *economies of scale*, in which scaled-up operations could lower unit costs. Resilient supply chains will be built on *economies of skill*. That's not merely a clever phrasing. It refers to four strategies you should employ to achieve resilient operations:

- Shift to outcome-based work
- Leverage global expertise
- Coevolve with lifelong learning
- Plan to build appropriate companywide skill sets

Do you pay employees for 40 hours per week of their time? Or do you pay them for outcomes? **Outcome-based work** is inherently more efficient because people have incentives to find new and faster solutions. Obviously this works best for white-collar roles, but blue-collar work can also be optimized, and for many functions the white/blue distinction is vanishing anyways. Certainly some roles will still need to be time-based, but that shouldn't be the default. Because when your company favors outcome-based work, you become more efficient not by scaling operations, but by being more skilled at them.

If your company has globally dispersed operations, do you need an expert at every site? Or do you need to empower a single undisputed expert to offer **global support**? Maybe she flies to a troubled site when needed. Maybe she has amazing online tools to offer remote support. Importantly, people at all your sites need to know who she is and what she can do. Expertise doesn't necessarily require economies of scale—you don't need to efficiently replicate her at every site. Instead, expertise requires economies of skill. You need to be efficient in taking advantage of her skills. Maybe she disseminates those skills through training. Or maybe you build a center of excellence around her.

For example, depending on your situation, you may want to embed net-zero culture across your organization. (We'll discuss why in Chapter 6.) Under the old lean principles, you needed economies of scale to produce lots of widgets inexpensively. Now you need economies of skill to learn how to produce widgets sustainably. You need new talent and capabilities, new business processes and engagement methodologies, new sources of data and decision rules. But every employee need not reinvent these wheels for themselves. Instead you develop expertise and encourage its spread.[13]

Your best renewable energy source is always people power. People want to learn, change, and grow. So your culture can and should encourage **lifelong learning**. If you present your employees with opportunities, many of them will want to develop capabilities *for themselves*. They don't necessarily need structured motivation such as incentives or career paths. They just need to know that they will learn something useful to them (not merely useful to the company) and that the process will be fun. This is the allure of gamification—even if in-game rewards don't mean much in the real world, they encourage these feelings of usefulness and fun.

(And because this is a hot topic, let's pause to examine it. By *gamification*, we mean creating personalized "challenges" associated with specific rewards. This can be a great way to boost engagement—for example, to keep people motivated to learn. However, it can be an obstacle when participants focus more on the rewards than the desired outcomes. For example, one company offered "points" for commenting on articles in an internal knowledge network; point-accumulating one-word comments

["Interesting"] ended up overwhelming the meaningful discussion/ learning that the company had intended to promote.)[14]

When you activate employees' lifelong learning, you become a *learning organization*. You thus become more resilient. You help employees turbocharge for success and confidently navigate change. You instill purpose in changing times.[15] This holds for both younger and older employees. Effective leaders need the ability to adapt their styles and expand their skill sets. In other words, they need to listen and learn, perhaps through tools such as town halls or reverse mentorships.[16]

There are many paths to becoming a learning organization: Maybe its most visible components are mentoring, guidance, lunch-and-learns, or other forms of relationship building. Maybe they're secondments or job rotations. Maybe they involve public rewards for taking risks and failing fast. Maybe leaders model an authentic commitment to learning. Regardless of form, your move to become a learning organization must involve a comprehensive, integrated strategy to embed the shift and sustain the new culture.[17]

Part of that strategy is setting a foundation for your future strengths. You need to know the challenges that might arise. For example, you probably don't need to build skill sets in fixing combustion engines. Instead, you **prioritize future skills needs** and then build well-rounded development programs to achieve them. By being transparent about the needs and opportunities, you are also improving your DEI agenda—previously underrepresented populations can see a clear path to make greater contributions to the firm.[18]

Human resources leaders have long encouraged their companies to become learning organizations. (See the sidebar, "Case Example: Driving Resilience by Upskilling Your Teams.") What has changed is that everyone should now more clearly see the benefits. Learning organizations are resilient: they see crises as opportunities to grow, on both the individual and corporate levels. These organizations are full of resilient people who can think out of the box. They have a stronger cross-functional perspective. As they get comfortable being uncomfortable, they become stress-resistant. When requirements or external conditions change, the people in learning organizations easily change with them.

## CASE EXAMPLE: DRIVING RESILIENCE BY UPSKILLING YOUR TEAMS

A leading global logistics company was a "beneficiary" of the COVID-19 pandemic. As everyone sat at home ordering things online, delivery services skyrocketed. Of course, an explosion of demand in the middle of a pandemic is hardly an unalloyed positive. Did the company have enough trucks? Did it have the warehouse space, technology, and operations expertise to efficiently handle the increased workloads? The shift came amid tumultuous changes in the industry. Service standards kept increasing, from two-day to next-day to same-day. Automation and other technological advances felt imminent, but required adjustments in processes, and didn't arrive everywhere all at once. New delivery modes included parcel lockers and alternative pick-up options such as retail stores.[19]

Thus amid all these pressures, one of the biggest questions was whether *people* at logistics companies could rise to the occasion. The industry had been traditionally plagued with high turnover rates. Employee demographics were heterogeneous: valuable veterans might extend their careers due to increased life expectancy, yet up to 50% of new hires were Generation Y, who came with different expectations of how to be managed. The company certainly needed more drivers—and good ones—to be its public face. It also needed sorters, loaders, and managers. And amid the fears of the pandemic, hiring wasn't easy.

This company took all the standard approaches. For example, it improved pay, benefits, and working conditions for employees. It celebrated these "essential workers" who helped everyday people survive the pandemic. It emphasized flexibility and resilience in management strategies.

However, it quickly saw that one of its best paths to resilience was to upskill its existing employees. Rather than throw a bunch of new hires into the fire, it could provide them with better training. Rather than hire new-to-the-company managers who understood how to work with new technologies, it could help existing employees gain those skills and earn promotions. Rather than letting frustrated employees leave, it could retain them with better career paths. Rather than letting less-skilled employees worry that robots would take their jobs, it could upskill them to work *with* robots at more value-added tasks.

The company realized that its conventional training methods and content were not adequately serving frontline supervisors and managers. But a patch was not enough. It needed to thoroughly reorganize its learning and development organizational structure. With the reboot, that function could develop a new mission and vision, new learning strategies, new guiding principles, and new curriculum frameworks.

Such a reorganization can be a multiyear process. But the company found a path to quick benefits with a *minimum viable product* approach. It identified roles with the most to gain, and the highest-priority technical and leadership skills those people needed. As it built a curriculum to address this niche, it included tools to systematically measure effectiveness, because the learning experience was not limited to the trainees. The organization itself would learn how to best facilitate learning.

One feature of the company's approach is to identify *learning journeys*. For key roles—which could be key steps in an employee's career—it identified the timing, depth of understanding, and delivery method for each learning outcome. For example, a supervisor needs managerial and leadership skills, plus business acumen. What combinations of classroom trainings, self-paced e-learning, on-the-job micro-learning, and other modalities could generate the right insights at the right time? When might gamification or virtual reality be particularly effective? How could micro-testing nudge learning on unknown concepts? What tools could best support social learning and peer-based advice? By developing answers to these questions *for each journey*, the company maximized the chances that its employees would increase their capabilities and career opportunities.

The company performed gap analyses to prioritize which journeys to develop first. Which modules could have the biggest impact on KPIs? Where had functional leaders identified training gaps? What were the biggest pain points for operations, and how could training address them? It then developed a variety of tools and activities to stimulate various types of learners. For example, it kept lecture components under 25%, mixing in plenty of activities. During virtual trainings, it encouraged chats, discussions, and breakouts to keep students engaged. It embraced a 70/20/10 approach to talent development, which professes that 70% of learning comes from on-the-job experiences, 20% from mentoring/relationships, and 10% from formal channels.

(*continued*)

(*continued*)

The results so far have included not only higher retention rates and more skilled employees—and not merely a company moving toward a more agile, adaptive, and accountable culture—but also employees with stronger leadership talents such as self-reliance. These *soft skills* give employees confidence that they can handle whatever life throws at them—which makes them more resilient. Furthermore, they gain vision into a long-term career path and development potential. That reduces turnover, making the workforce as a whole more resilient.

CHAPTER 5

# Principle 4:
## Enable Resilience Through Technology by Combining Human Judgment with Artificial Intelligence

### Warehouses Demonstrate Coming Technology Trends

Lots of people don't think much about warehouses. They're huge, nondescript buildings, now often called *distribution centers*, near highway exits. For the past decade, however, warehouses have participated in constant revolutions in digital technology. The warehousing function has transformed, and will continue to transform.

It's a fascinating story of what technology can do. Similar technological changes will transform many industries, perhaps including your own. But more important, it's a fascinating story of technological changes in *a key component of your supply chain*. Similar technological changes will soon transform the rest of your supply chain—these changes are too powerful to ignore.

For decades, warehouses were merely a holding point before products were shipped to customers. Their inventory represented money wasting away by the minute. The building and real estate were also expenses to be minimized. You wanted a plain, cheap building. You wanted it out of town where land was cheap. And you wanted to maximize inventory turns in a space as small as possible.

Then some online retailers (okay, mostly Amazon) started operating for the consumer. They offered faster delivery times and wider assortments of products. And consumers proved insatiable. They wanted ever-more stuff, ever faster. Warehouses became more of a productive strategic resource that could flex to absorb demand volatility. A company now needs its network of warehouses to operate like a dam and sluice, regulating the flow of goods in nimble response to surges and drops in demand. If your warehouses aren't perfectly located and operating perfectly, you can't fulfill orders and meet customer expectations.[1]

Thus the emergence of new kinds of warehouses. E-commerce fulfillment centers feature high ceilings and multiple mezzanine floors. Hybrid stores devote part of their space to in-store shoppers and part to online order fulfillment and returns processing. Dark stores are closed urban retail locations now entirely dedicated to last-mile delivery. All of these variations involve smaller orders than the pallet-sized loads of the traditional warehouse. All are more complex and expensive.

Direct-to-consumer fulfillment means that warehouse product flows and replenishment become more complicated and labor-intensive. E-commerce consumers return more items, which means that operations need to account for reverse logistics. And since the pandemic, many firms are holding greater safety stock. Amid this rising complexity, the always-tight warehousing labor market still sees annual turnover of 43%.

In short, warehouses need resilience. And the best path to get there involves technology. (See the sidebar, "Technology Transforms Warehouse Operations.")

Because warehouses are so complicated, potentially problematic, and strategically vital, some consumer packaged goods and retail companies are insourcing them. Others are demanding that their third-party logistics providers (3PLs) step up their capabilities to play a more strategic role.

## TECHNOLOGY TRANSFORMS WAREHOUSE OPERATIONS

Warehouse operations are all about moving products. Products arrive, get placed on a shelf, get picked for an order, and then leave. You can have people with forklifts moving all this stuff. But the work isn't interesting, well paying, consistent, or particularly safe. It's great for robots and automation.

To move the products themselves, large warehouses often invest in shuttle systems. Smaller warehouses may prefer automated guided vehicles (AGVs) or autonomous mobile robots (AMRs). But how do you efficiently pick items for an order? Once, a person had to trek to far-flung corners of the warehouse. Now, the AMRs and AGVs can help. Alternatively, you can bring the inventory to the order picker, with technology solutions including carousels, vertical lifts, automated storage and retrieval systems, mini-loads, and automated material-carrying vehicles. Rather than investing in lots of physical robots, many warehouses are buying robotics as a service (RaaS). This model helps warehouses shift capital expenses (capex) to operating expenses (opex), which often brings advantages in flexibility, income taxes, and cashflow. RaaS also requires less infrastructure and scales up and down with seasonal trends.

But a warehouse can't just store products. It also has to know where they are. Shippers and third-party logistics providers (3PLs) want to track their products in real time. They thus call on warehouses to invest in internet-enabled sensors (the Internet of Things) and radio frequency identification (RFID). In the "cold chain"—for perishables and pharmaceuticals with temperature requirements—sensors monitor time and temperature of pallets. To take inventory, some warehouses use drones that take advantage of 5G-enabled indoor positioning systems.

That's a lot of technology, and to manage it, warehouses need more technology. A traditional warehouse management system (WMS) is now often supplemented with a warehouse execution system (WES). The amount of information flowing through the warehouse has expanded exponentially (in part because there's also now information about the technology itself). That's what a WES manages.

The story of warehouses is one of lean principles (*Keep costs down! Keep inventories low!*) colliding with risk management (*More safety stock! More agility!*). The technology helps: it moves items and provides information. But the real value is created when the technology is combined with the human capacity for creative thinking, sound judgment, and crisis management.[2]

Private equity funds such as Bain Capital Real Estate are heavily investing in space, and venture capitalists such as Lux Capital and Khosla Ventures are investing in technology and automation solutions beyond robotics.[3]

In short, although warehousing may not be a high-profile sector of the economy, it's at the forefront of many technological changes. Companies are faced with choices of where and how much to invest in robotics and artificial intelligence (AI). But the environment isn't static. The main challenge comes in wondering whether a solution you say yes to today will still be relevant when it's ready in a year or two—and consumers have moved on.

For this reason, we are always encouraging companies to focus not on technology itself, but what the technology can do. That's why AI and machine learning (ML) are so exciting: what they can do is learn. You're not just buying this technology to solve today's problems. You're buying it to learn and solve tomorrow's problems.

But again, let's focus on the outcome rather than the technology itself. What you want is learning, constant learning. To achieve resilience, your organization needs to constantly learn. And although AI/ML show promise at learning, humans are already really good at it. So maybe, at least within your company, the distinction between AI and HI (human intelligence) is overblown. It's going to be the *combination* of AI and HI that will help warehouses—and indeed all operations functions in all companies. They will improve resilience not just by investing in technology but also by investing in constant learning.

## Transparency Improves Resilience

In an ideal world, you would have real-time visibility into every aspect of your supply chain. You could watch the product being built, noticing any crises in real time. You could watch the goods flowing through your transportation networks, into your warehouses, and then out again to your customers. You could even watch your customers interact with the product. After all, if automobiles can tell insurance companies about people's driving habits, why can't all sorts of products tell their manufacturers about how they're being used?

One key to resilience is transparency: the ability to detect that something has gone wrong. The more you can "see" into your supply chain, the more quickly you can act to forestall a crisis. And the broader you define those boundaries—from consumer use all the way back to raw material suppliers—the more resilience you gain. Whatever you seek to do—automate, break down silos, or apply constant learning—it starts with transparency.

Of course, full transparency is impossible. But today's digital signals can bring you far closer to it than ever before. The IoT provides sensors everywhere: in products, in pallets, in warehouses, or at tier 2 or 3 suppliers. Amid the pandemic, with retail outlets closing and online demand growing, Nike used RFID tags to track a billion units of footwear and apparel. "We were able to leverage the inventory visibility in order to be able to take advantage of . . . the demand that we had across the marketplace and across our retail stores," CFO Matthew Friend said on an earnings call.[4]

Meanwhile, the 5G wireless standard (and, coming soon, 6G) helps transmit massive amounts of information. For example, to address "leakage" of misplaced pallets in its warehouses, which can account for 5 to 10% of inventory, Maersk deploys autonomous drones to fly through warehouses. It then uses video analytics and AI to process the drones' images, videos, and 3D scans looking for missing pallets. The result: leakage has been nearly eliminated.[5]

Indeed, supply chains are likely to follow other sectors of the economy in massive digitization. Since 2009, Amazon Web Services (AWS) has gone from zero to $90 billion in revenues, largely because industries such as finance and entertainment wanted to digitize everything (and store that digital information on AWS servers). Operating in a fully digital environment helped these industries unleash new sets of capabilities. Why wouldn't this also happen to supply chains? Planning, order taking, connecting to suppliers—all can be fully digitized, which will unleash new sets of capabilities. They start with transparency. The only question is how these massive amounts of information will be structured and governed. (See the sidebar, "Don't Call It Blockchain!")

## DON'T CALL IT BLOCKCHAIN!

*Distributed ledger* is the generic name for the technology behind blockchain—and thus behind cryptocurrencies, non-fungible tokens (NFTs), the alleged "genius" of Sam Bankman-Fried, and all sorts of other fantastical stories. But *distributed ledger* also has a more prosaic, arguably more useful, application in supply chains.

The operation of a supply chain is now bogged down by many tedious and inefficient manual processes: signatures, verifications, inspections, dispute resolutions, and more. Sensors and other technologies can help, but how is that information stored and processed? The distributed ledger—a blockchain—could provide the decentralization and transparency to radically reduce logistics inefficiencies. Imagine executing bills of lading using blockchain technology: you could prevent forgeries and documentation delays. Imagine a blockchain-driven data exchange open to all stakeholders along the supply chain: you could gain radical transparency.

However, there are huge problems in implementing this idea, especially because it requires up front a great deal of trust. (It's ironic, because cryptocurrencies were once advertised as *eliminating* the need for trust. Then again . . .) To achieve genuine efficiency, you'd want all companies and governments to agree ahead of time that the system would work. It's hard to gain that trust, given that making all data in a network transparent to all users can undermine trade secrets. There are also technical issues. For example, a smart contract won't self-execute without connectivity at the point of delivery to log the fact that the goods were delivered. Most of the technical issues are solvable, but would require a great deal of collaboration. It's hard to get parties with conflicting agendas to collaborate, so solutions are likely far in the future.[6]

Pilot projects show promise. For example, beginning in 2019, Walmart Canada developed a private blockchain to automate invoices from and payments to its 70 third-party freight carriers. Walmart and its carriers aligned their interests: Walmart gains transparency into information, and carriers gain timely payments and better reconciliation. Previously, more than 70% of invoices were disputed; the blockchain solution cuts that to less than 1%.[7] The disadvantage is that these benefits are limited to this small network. And while many pilots have been attempted dating back to the mid-2010s, few have gained much momentum in today's ever-changing world.

Will blockchain transform supply chains? A few years ago, we were cautiously optimistic. Despite the hurdles, this technology fits well with other emerging transformative technologies. But the public travails of blockchain-associated trends may give the underlying technology an unwarranted bad name. That could only add to the hurdles rather than tearing them down.

Gaining the benefits of digitization and transparency—with or without blockchain—requires a great deal of trust. Your suppliers should not perceive transparency as a mandate or a punishment. (They don't want Big Brother looking over their shoulders any more than your employees do.) Rather, as we discussed in Chapter 2, this is part of a move toward increased partnerships with your suppliers. You are buying from them not just supplies but supplies *and information*. You will want them to understand the benefits of this information. And you may well need to compensate them for it.

## Technology Creates New, Resilient Business Models

We are amid a gigantic change in the landscape of manufacturing and production. Compared to the advent of the internet, or social media, it may be less visible to the average consumer. But it is still a set of profound changes that you should harness for the sake of resilience.

We're speaking, first, of the so-called *fourth industrial revolution* (i4.0). Digital technologies such as robotics and artificial intelligence are already reshaping every stage of the production cycle. Soon the physical, digital, and biological worlds will intersect in unprecedented ways, spawning both opportunity and peril. Here are the five most transformative technologies:

- The IoT
- AI
- Advanced robotics
- Wearables
- 3D printing

For example, the IoT is not just "devices talking to each other." It's devices providing essential information to key business functions, such as enterprise planning, scheduling, and product–life cycle systems. SKF, a global bearing manufacturer, now offers a predictive maintenance solution for industrial machines, called SKF Axios, powered by AWS. The solution is based on IoT sensors and ML capabilities that improve machine reliability and notify users when something goes wrong.[8] AI is not just for generating subpar marketing text for free. It's for learning and acting on customer activities faster and more accurately, as well as improving production through predictive maintenance, process optimization, and improved quality management. Wearable technology may well represent the next major computing platform, the true successor to handheld and other devices. For example, wearables could accelerate worker training, enhance productivity, and improve safety. And you can integrate 3D printers with other shop-floor production systems, complementing conventional manufacturing systems. This combination can achieve mass customization, as well as producing low-volume, high-value parts such as aerospace equipment, medical instruments, and tooling.

As they converge—more swiftly than many realize—these technologies will give rise to a "factory of the future." Costs will plummet, efficiency will increase, and high-quality, quick-turnaround "batches of one" will become feasible. For example, we named the Siemens Smart Infrastructure plant in Zug, Switzerland, 2022 Factory of the Year in the category "Excellence in supply chain resilience." The plant makes components for fire detectors and other building automation systems. Its agile demand forecasting interacts with supply planning for quick adaptation. It continuously monitors more than 1,500 suppliers and external data such as weather forecasts to predict risk events and their potential impacts. It uses market intelligence to proactively calculate proper safety stocks.[9]

This convergence of technologies will open new avenues for the creation of customized and connected products, as well as novel business models such as pay-per-performance. Yet to realize the full value of such developments, you will need to innovatively collaborate with suppliers and other partners. You will strengthen your supply chain to achieve resilience.[10]

New frontiers of manufacturing are cool. What's profitable is when they support new business models. Do your customers *want* batch sizes of one? Can wearables or robots free your employees to create value in exciting new ways? Can 3D printing accelerate your reshoring efforts? These are not merely gee-whiz technologies. They are opportunities to rethink your supply chains and ideas of resilience.

For example, consider a pair of the most-talked-about companies of the last decade: Uber and Airbnb. They are famously mere platforms to connect buyers and sellers of rides and lodging. They don't have a supply chain—they don't have to build hotel rooms or lease fleets of taxis. Except that, effectively, they *do* have supply chains that deliver the desired goods and services (on time and with sufficient quality). They just used technology to rethink their business models, and rethink their supply chains.

Indeed, during the pandemic, Airbnb did so again. When COVID-19 severely curtailed demand for short-term leisure lodging, Airbnb focused on new customer needs. For example, people wanted to escape crowded cities for extended stays in more remote locations, or be closer to family members to help them through a prolonged crisis. By rethinking its business model, and its lodging "supply chain," Airbnb increased business volumes comparable to pre-COVID levels. This resilience positioned Airbnb not only to weather the current storm but also to grow new markets.[11]

Crisis equals opportunity, as the old saying goes. Technology-empowered resilience creates the capability to then *take advantage* of opportunities by adjusting business models. Consider A.P. Moller-Maersk, the ocean shipping giant. It sees the increased role that technology will play in logistics—the value of transparency as discussed in the previous section ("Transparency Improves Resilience"). It has invested in digital freight technologies. Yet once it has a strength in those technologies, it can transform its business model to be an end-to-end provider, a one-stop-shop for shippers. It can diversify its portfolio away from the boom-and-bust cycles of ocean shipping toward the more value-added activities often summarized as *freight forwarding*. In pursuit of that goal, it subsequently acquired numerous logistics companies (including warehouses, yielding the drone example cited previously). Maersk may or may not achieve the goal—freight forwarding is a crowded, competitive market. But if it does, it will be gaining resilience against threats to ocean shipping.

## Automation Improves Resilience

Across a broad range of supply chain activities, technology is finally ready to replace human labor. In the previous section ("Technology Creates New, Resilient Business Models"), we discussed some of these marvelous new technologies. Here, we'd like to focus on the way they can *automate* work and production. After all, the factor that drove your supply chains to become so far-flung and brittle was that you had all this work to do, and you needed people who would do it cheaply. What if you didn't have to do the work? You would gain opportunities to operate where you choose.

This is what these new technologies promise. If you have robots applying the weld, you don't have people doing so. If you have IoT sensors sending the information, 3D printers making the part, drones finding the missing inventory, and AI analyzing the situation, your decisions no longer have to be constrained by the price or availability of labor. You can choose to do this work wherever you want. You can reshore to be closer to customers; you can continue manufacturing abroad because their managers have accumulated great expertise; you can move the factory away from a hurricane-prone area; you can even put it next to the CEO's house because she wants a short commute. Automation frees you to make strategic decisions based on your priorities.

Automation is not a panacea. It's especially valuable for manufacturing in high labor cost markets with aging demographics—but you may not need to manufacture in such markets. Implementing it may require training; for example, AI solutions such as ChatGPT may be able to help employees to become more efficient, but only if they know how to use it. Yet employees—and customers—may resist this and other forms of automation. It creates attack surfaces for cyber threats. It creates its own dependencies, especially for things such as spare parts or cheap energy. So you certainly need to apply it judiciously.

But the potential gigantic benefit—especially for AI—is to separate prediction from judgment. You have an opportunity to rebalance machine intelligence with human agency.[12] Because so much public attention goes to AI in standalone services such as autonomous driving, it's worth repeating this point: the real promise of AI is in *complementing* HI. For example, take *cobots*—robots that interact directly with humans. They combine AI with HI to lower labor costs in manufacturing facilities.

On factory floors, humans continue to do most of the work in manufacturing operations—72% of the tasks, according to a Kearney/Drishti survey, which contribute 71% of the value created. After all, humans can reason, adapt, and innovate. The problem is that humans can be inconsistent. That can lead to costly defects. That's where cobots can help—by taking on jobs that require repetitive movements and/or by augmenting quality control at the end of the manufacturing line. It's also where AI can help: by analyzing massive amounts of data all across the line.[13]

Thus, rather than remove human beings completely, you want to free them to do what they do best: make critical judgments based on their experience and expertise. They can investigate and learn from system failures. They can make things better, rather than doing the same things again and again. If a pattern is stable, then a machine can do it. But in picking up a book about resilience, you're acknowledging that patterns are often unstable. That's where humans are needed. Every time you begin a new product or market or customer segment, you need human judgment. That judgment may be augmented by AI predictions, but AI is better at executing tasks than thinking about the big picture.[14] It's the AI/HI combination that does the constant learning and that makes your operations more resilient.

## Learning Improves Resilience

The real transformational possibilities arise when you're able to combine technologies—and combine them with HI. People will learn from AI, and vice versa. AI will analyze IoT data and inform robots or cobots. Processes will be transformed, and new products and economies of scale will emerge. But you must always be asking, What is the role of people at each stage of this flow? What type of people do we need? And are these people available for us to hire?

Because in the end, what you want isn't a fully automated operation. That's not necessarily resilient. What you want is a constantly learning organization. The ability to learn is what will enable you to respond to crises, adapt to changing customer preferences, and profit from innovations. Technology can assist in such learning: wearables and other sensors provide lots of information, AI helps analyze it, 3D printers turn it into mass customization, and so on. But it's people who learn. People have a hunger to learn, people can ask questions of technological tools to learn more intelligently, and people have the creativity and flexibility to learn more broadly.

Resilience results not from technology itself, but from the learning that technology can enable. It's the combination of human judgment and technological tools that achieves resilience. (See the sidebar, "Case Example: Making Better Decisions Through End-To-End Transparency and Demand Sensing.") Chapter 4 describes the needed changes in your people and organization; now we've seen how to incorporate technology into those changes. In Chapter 6 we'll look at making them sustainable over the long term.

---

**CASE EXAMPLE: MAKING BETTER DECISIONS THROUGH END-TO-END TRANSPARENCY AND DEMAND SENSING**

A pharmacy retailer with thousands of outlets was facing inventory challenges. The old lean rules had suggested a just-in-time inventory philosophy, but the risks of a volatile world made that just too dangerous. Its customers were often suffering and needed immediate relief, so it couldn't afford stock-outs. However, a just-in-case inventory philosophy cost too much. It tied up working capital. It didn't make productive use of store space. Its historical view failed to account for the varying ways that customers shifted to online purchases in certain categories. Could data and analytics help?

The company's first step was to get its data in order. For example, did it have the numbers to understand a product's past sales performance by location? Did it know in-stock rates and shipping lead times? Could it track pricing and promotions? Was all of the data reliable? How close was it to real time? Were collection processes consistent? Where were the anomalies? (There are always anomalies. The company wanted to understand them, so it could factor them into decisions.)

Then it started working on connections and new data sources. It built an AI/ML-enabled platform, leveraging its full scope of data. It built the expertise to develop algorithms to run on that data and make predictions. It explored additional test datasets and model results to incorporate into that data warehouse. And it invested in tools for end users in internal departments to explore hypotheses.

This kind of flywheel can take some time to get moving. The company developed and refined use cases. It ran experiments, and then reran them with additional key performance indicators (KPIs) or data fields. It included additional weeks of available data. As the strength of its models improved, it added granularity. Then it explored how to treat edge use cases.

It used the algorithms to answer questions such as, what external factors might drive a product's sales? For example, it considered reviews at various online sites—how did they affect sales in the physical store? Similarly, how were sales affected by, for example, a sudden increase in Google searches for words like *antiseptic* or *antibacterial*?

Which of the old ways of doing business were driving suboptimal levels of safety stock? Was it the set and forget mentality? The lack of business rules and governance? Unadjusted defaults? A bias toward certain results such as on time in full? How might inventory management be adjusted to better align with business objectives?

It took time to develop business rules that algorithms could use to automate controls. Time, and plenty of human intervention. The company started with numerous manually controlled parameters, such as minimum and maximum levels of safety stock. AI would merely trigger human review of a situation. As the system learned, it could start recommending adjustments to individual parameters on the item/location level, with a summary of such recommendations provided to a human for approval.

(*continued*)

(*continued*)

Within six months, the company saw productivity improvements in inventory. But it's also pleased that its platform has a road map for key process changes, exception-driven reporting, and centralized governance of replenishment parameters. Much fine-tuning remains. The company will continue to improve the way it makes decisions based on these inputs. And it clearly will explore new areas to apply AI insights. But for now, its flywheel is moving, and that movement has energized its operations.

CHAPTER 6

# Principle 5:
## Ensure Long-Term Resilience by Embracing Sustainability

### The Chemicals Industry Illustrates the Far-Reaching Implications of Sustainability

Corporate boards around the world are taking action on sustainability and decarbonization. They have established (if not always fully empowered) initiatives to address environmental, social, and governance (ESG) issues. We assume that, as a corporate leader, you're on board with these imperatives—if you're not, yet, please see the sidebar, "Why ESG Is Strategic, Not Political."

Our job here, then, is to show the link between sustainability and resilient operations. Why does your long-term resilience require you to embrace sustainability? What does that look like? And does it really hold for every company? To accomplish that job, we're going to start with a story about the chemicals industry. If you don't work in chemicals, you may find it an obscure industry—and certainly not central to sustainability. But that's part of our point: sustainability is essential to resilience in all industries. And now is the time to act.

## WHY ESG IS STRATEGIC, NOT POLITICAL

If you're a CEO, you could be forgiven for thinking that *sustainability* is a political topic. When smart people have tried to explain it, they have often given you an acronym salad—SBTs, COP26, GRI, SDGs—instead of taking the time to think from your perspective.[1] So let's set aside the technical details and focus on what's relevant: the world has changed, and your strategy needs to keep up.

The world has changed in two ways. First, people now care about carbon impacts. And when we say *people*, we mean *your customers*. Also your employees. And your funders. In other words, pretty much all of your stakeholders. *Customers* now understand the negative externalities of globalization, and they will pay more for sustainable products.[2] Talented *employees* now believe their choices will affect their grandchildren's lives, and they prefer to work for sustainability-oriented companies.[3] And *funders* such as BlackRock now want to see the business plan by which you will achieve net-zero carbon emissions by 2050.[4]

Notice that we didn't mention government regulators. They too do now care about sustainability. But you shouldn't approach sustainability thinking, "*I need to satisfy government regulators*." Why? Because that's the old, outdated view: sustainability as a political topic. Sustainability is no longer something debated in op-ed pages and legislative hearings. It's now a strategic topic. It's influencing your customers, employees, and funders—and thus needs to influence how you operate in the world.

Many climate advocates are still stuck in the political world. They harp on how you should save the planet. And it's easy to respond, frustrated, "Look, we all want to save the planet, but it'd be a lot easier if the incentives lined up." Here's the good news: the incentives now line up! In today's world, even if you didn't *want* to save the planet, you would need a strategy to reduce carbon emissions because your *customers* want to (also your employees, your funders, and your regulators). The incentives are now telling you that what you already want to do—make your operations more environmentally sustainable—can lead to increased profits.

The second way the world has changed is in risk. Because the climate is changing, your operations face new and greater risks. Floods, wildfires, hurricanes, dust storms—the list grows longer every year. Climate events destroy assets and disrupt operations across your entire value chain, from tier 3 suppliers to last-mile consumer delivery.

> But note that the sources of today's increased universe of risks are not only environmental. They're also social. Here's the oft-overlooked, hard-to-quantify *S* component of your ESG agenda. What if one of your suppliers is exposed as using slave labor? What if a key input comes from a politically reprehensible or war-torn state? What if a customer, employee, or funder wants to understand how the diversity of your suppliers reflects your customer or employee base? Given that the implications of these crises could play out in courtrooms, in lost revenue, or on social media, the risks are indeed high.
>
> These are arguments for action on *sustainability* (defined broadly, to include the socially sustainable). They are also arguments for why you need operations resilience. And that's the point of this chapter: action on sustainability improves long-term resilience.

In the chemical industry, many companies have grasped the need to address greenhouse gas (GHG) emissions. As you may know, the GHG Protocol has divided emissions into three scopes. It's easy for corporate leaders to see the value of addressing scope 1 (emissions caused by the company itself) and scope 2 (indirect emissions from purchased electricity, heating and cooling, and so on). But many companies incorrectly view scope 3 (indirect emissions upstream and downstream of company's operations) as a more distant, less urgent problem.

In fact, scope 3 requires immediate analysis and action. As demands to reduce carbon come from customers, regulators, and investors, chemical companies are realizing that at least 75% of their emissions come from scope 3. To reduce emissions, chemical companies need to address purchased materials that account for almost half of scope 3 emissions.

Why must a chemical company focus on scope 3? Again, there's a political answer and a strategic answer. Politically, the Science Based Targets Initiative is developing guidance for scope 3 target-setting methods and criteria through 2023. It is also developing specifics for decarbonization in the chemicals industry and various subsectors. The US Securities and Exchange Commission has also proposed that companies publish their scope 3 emissions as part of their financial reporting process. None of these initiatives are developing as quickly as they were expected to in 2022. Everyone involved is recognizing the scope of the challenge. But they still represent political priorities.

Regulators are focused on scope 3 because the decarbonization problem is holistic. If the world focuses only on scope 1, reprehensible-but-powerful companies (your competitors?!) could rejigger their operations to exclude carbon-emitting activities from their "responsibilities." For example, an oil company could argue that gasoline doesn't emit much carbon until after it has been sold to a consumer. Technically, each individual car driver has the scope 1 responsibility—even though, of course, individual car drivers lack the scale and market power to do much about it. The way to solve the holistic problem is to encourage every company to be responsible for emissions across its entire value chain. Activists know this. They know it's more effective to pressure Apple to reduce its scope 3 emissions than it is to pressure the manufacturer of a tiny endpiece for an iPhone cord to be responsible for its scope 1 emissions. And if these trends are going to affect Apple, and oil companies, then they're also going to affect more obscure companies, such as those in the chemicals industry. These pressures thus create some degree of political imperative.

But there are also strategic reasons for a chemicals executive to focus on scope 3 emissions. You face supply risks. What if your supplier of emissions-intensive materials gets shut down, due to these intensifying political pressures? Will you have sufficient qualified sources to substitute? And what if the supplier of a more sustainable, reasonably priced alternative needs a little help scaling up production—and one of your competitors has offered that help? Why would they sell to you?

These dynamics are now playing out in chemicals. Executives are learning a lot about decarbonization pathways so as to find opportunities to reduce emissions. For example, let's say you make plastics. Your scope 3 emissions thus include those of the supplier that produces your propylene. When propylene is made from coal as the feedstock, Kearney estimates that average global emissions are 12 kilograms of carbon dioxide equivalent per kilogram. That's 2.5 times higher than when the propylene is made from naphtha, and 6.5 times higher than when it's made from methanol. With plant-specific emissions data—and cost comparisons—chemicals companies can identify opportunities to reduce scope 3 emissions.[5]

Of course, propylene is just one example. A chemicals company—similar to any other company—will have many products, each with multiple pathways to decarbonization, and with some of those pathways not yet clearly defined. For example, to decarbonize ammonia production, do you switch feedstocks or pursue carbon capture, utilization, and sequestration (CCUS)? Right now, with zero-emission ammonia feedstocks still at lab scale, CCUS seems the safer option. But there are risks to moving either too fast *or* too slow—and those risks vary depending on your corporate culture. If you commit to being a first mover, you're willing to invest in production technology while it is still relatively high on the cost curve. But if your company has a slower-moving culture, overcoming cost concerns will be a significant undertaking.

Furthermore, you need good data. But will your suppliers be willing to provide this data? It may cause them to lose sales to same-cost, lower-emission competitors. Specialty data services can overcome the data gap, and sometimes you can even customize these databases to show plant-specific emissions rates by manufacturer. But not all data is created equal. It would really be best to be collaborating productively with your suppliers.

In short, we're getting back to the themes of previous chapters. You build operations resilience through collaboration and trust across the supply chain. This holds true whether you're building short-term resilience against logistics disruptions or long-term resilience based on sustainability.

Resilience implies sustainability. Sustainability implies resilience. The two go hand-in-hand. For long-term resilience, you need a sustainable strategy. (See the sidebar, "A Sustainability Strategy? Or a Sustainable Strategy?") Such a strategy is straightforward to design and implement.

## A SUSTAINABILITY STRATEGY? OR A SUSTAINABLE STRATEGY?

If *sustainability* were only a political issue, you would need to address it with a *sustainability strategy*. This would likely be a plan to get to net-zero emissions and a diversified supply base and workforce by some future date. It might (or might not) satisfy advocates. It might (or might not) be something that your operations team would pay attention to.

But because sustainability is a *strategic* issue, you need a broader strategy. You need a way to drive *the sustainable* deep into your organization's values. You need a strategy that will sustain you through wildfires and other climate events, through human-trafficking scandals, social unrest, and political nightmares.

You need to *mitigate* and *adapt*. For example, you want to mitigate climate change by reducing your carbon footprint. But you also want to adapt to climate change by having a backup plan in case your preferred port gets flooded. Likewise, you should mitigate social injustice by hiring more diverse suppliers. And you also want to adapt to the risks of a socially aware world by, for example, gaining visibility into how your tier 3 suppliers treat the people who pick the cotton that goes into your products.

In this context, *adaptation* is the process of adjusting to the current and future effects of climate change and social justice. On the climate side, most corporate initiatives today are too heavily indexed on mitigation. Only 10% of climate investment is directed at adaptation. Yet adaptation is resilience. Here's your chance to differentiate.[6]

# To Promote Resilience, Sustainability Must Be a Strategy Not a Silo

As sustainability has become trendy in the past few years, it's been tempting to respond half-heartedly. Sure, we'll fill out this checkbox for compliance. Sure, we'll create an office of sustainability. Sure, we'll put recycling bins in the marketing office. But let's not let this distract from our main purpose! Yet as the previous discussion shows, whatever your main purpose is, sustainability is fully interwoven with it. It's not something you bolt on to existing operations.

Sustainability is a holistic balance among economic, environmental, and social factors. It arises from core values that dictate a philosophy of sustainable operations. Those core values are what give you resilience. And the resilience gives you market power. Sustainability creates competitive advantage. For example, a 2019 study for Coca-Cola found that its supplier diversity initiatives led to favorable perceptions among consumers, which would cause an additional 670,000 consumers to more frequently consume the company's products.[7]

So you can approach sustainability just like you would any other business strategy. Two of us helped write an entire book about this, *The Sustainability Chessboard*.[8] To briefly summarize the process:

1. **Baseline.** First you need to understand where you are. How much do you want to do about sustainability, and how good are you at actually doing it?
2. **Target.** Next you need to understand where you're going. What are the sustainability targets you want to achieve, and what's the path to get there?
3. **Road map.** Now you translate ambition into action. Break the targets down into a road map with tasks specific to each unit and function.
4. **Implement.** Now you do the work. Each department identifies the levers or actions that it needs to put into practice. Then it does so and reports back on results.
5. **Evaluate.** The sum of all reports shows you whether you're on track.

Obviously this is a highly simplified summary of a potentially complicated initiative. (That's why we wrote *The Sustainability Chessboard*!) Is your ambition to better leverage current sustainability data, to create more value through sustainability, or to lead sustainability innovation in your sector? These varying strategies dictate the approaches you can take—from improving data collection and analysis to embracing circular business models. Each approach has varying levers you can pull—from sustainability benchmarking to big data–based end-to-end sustainability footprint tracking.

We're not saying, *This is easy*. We're saying, *This is familiar*. The benefits and pitfalls of developing a sustainability strategy resemble the benefits and pitfalls of developing any other business strategy. If you're good at doing strategy, you'll be good at this. If you're not good at doing strategy, then you've got bigger problems than achieving long-term resilience through sustainability.

## Some Examples of Sustainable Resilience Strategies

Let's say that, inspired by this chapter, you want to develop a strategy to address scope 3 emissions. Your tasks roughly follow the ones we just identified:

1. **Baseline.** Use available data to understand your current emissions. Identify hot spots.
2. **Targets.** Set near-term and long-term target emissions. One approach would be to analyze your product portfolio to see what are the cradle-to-grave highest-emitting products. You may need to engage your customers and suppliers to obtain data on emissions during product use.
3. **Road map.** How are you going to reach the targets? One approach would be to analyze and segment suppliers to create targeted interaction models. Also, how are you going to measure your work? You can identify digital enablers (such as data or software) that can measure and track your carbon footprint and reduction efforts.
4. **Implement.** Step 3 should have resulted in a portfolio of projects. Choose the most promising and get them done.
5. **Evaluate.** What did you get done, and what did you learn?

A word about that portfolio of projects: it's not that you will choose the *easy* rather than *hard*, or even the *high ROI* over the *low ROI*. We like to talk about how sustainability projects span *levels of transformation* (see Figure 6.1). Some projects (labeled A in the figure) can be addressed by your purchasing organization. The B projects may require end-to-end innovation across your organization, but will lead to more significant benefits. The C projects will involve your full ecosystem of suppliers and customers, perhaps leading you to new business models—and new growth.

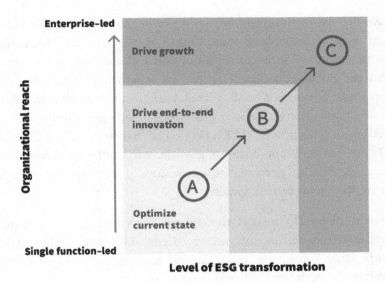

Enterprise-led

Organizational reach

Drive growth

Drive end-to-end
innovation

Optimize
current state

Single function-led

**Level of ESG transformation**

Ⓒ **Business growth:**
Radical business model/ecosystem transformation
(customers, competitors, regulators, industry bodies, and so on)

Ⓑ **Operational innovation:**
New networks, suppliers, technologies

Ⓐ **Current state:**
Existing networks, suppliers, products

**Figure 6.1**   Portfolio of sustainability projects
*Source:* Kearney analysis.

The three types of projects are *not* sequential. You need not—should
not—wait to optimize A before beginning B and C. Why? Because the
complex B and C projects will require sustained, multiyear efforts. They need
to gain a perch, now, in organizations outside of purchasing, such as R&D,
product management, marketing, manufacturing, supply chain, and finance.[9]

As a third example, let's look at sustainability in fast fashion. In
Chapter 3, we highlighted fast fashion as an example of creating resilience by creating value for customers—although we noted that this
model has big sustainability problems. How to rectify the two?

We believe that coming disruptions will move the fashion industry toward more sustainable models. One is the secondhand opportunity: consumers now see secondhand shopping as smart, cool, and sustainable. At first, the global secondhand market was dominated by pure *re-commerce* players (most famously ThredUp, Poshmark, and the RealReal, although there are many others). But as it grows, big brands are entering the space (including, among others, H&M, Levi's, The North Face, and Patagonia).

There are different business models, with different strengths and weaknesses. But in general, fashion brands gain three benefits from entering the secondhand market:

- Own the brand's narrative throughout the entire consumer journey. Similar to automakers entering the used-car market (GM's CarBravo, Ford's Blue Advantage, etc.), apparel makers can control favorable positioning in the secondhand market.
- Build a deeper relationship with consumers. Brands can capture valuable insights by reconnecting with consumers at the end of the garment's life—when the consumers are now the sellers.
- Tap into new consumer segments. Consumers who were either unwilling or unable to afford new high-end items may become fans of a brand by buying secondhand first.[10]

But secondhand is only a preview of a broader disruption to come: circularity. After all, real change can only be achieved when sustainability is accounted for at every stage of the value chain. That means encouraging consumers to buy fewer clothes in the first place, and then keep them for longer. Kearney's Circular Fashion Index (CFX) measures fashion brands' efforts to extend the life cycle of their clothes. Although many brands score quite poorly, Patagonia, The North Face, and Levi's boast promise:

- They communicate openly that their products should last longer.
- They encourage consumers to drop off their old clothes in a store, incentivizing them with coupons or discounts. (The dropped-off clothes are either sold secondhand or recycled.)
- They increase the amount of recycled fabrics, such as polyester or cotton, that they use in their products.

- They offer repair and maintenance of clothes.
- Each increased its score from 2020, when the CFX debuted, to 2022.
- Each company pairs its sustainability improvements with sound financial performance.

Again, the fashion industry's overall circularity scores have been abysmal. But these three companies, and occasional examples elsewhere, show that progress is possible. Design, education, monofibers, materials sourcing: there are many immediate actions that any brand could take. Indeed, at least across Europe, many brands are already taking one or more such actions. They just need to be more consistent and holistic.[11]

Because—and here's where we get back to resilience—assuming consumer sentiment continues to shift toward ethical and sustainable lifestyles, this means an opportunity. Circularity already shows signs of being the next disruptive force in fashion. Regulations are coming, at least in Europe and some US states. Google searches for sustainable fashion are up by 350%. Many other brands are at least marginally improving their CFX scores. When the circularity disruption hits the industry, those players will be better positioned for competitive advantage. And when circularity hits other industries—for example, Whirli is a UK-based subscription platform for borrowing and swapping toys—some companies will be better-prepared than others.

## Additional Angles for Sustainability as a Strategy

In this chapter, we're arguing that embracing sustainability will help you be resilient in the long term. We've shown how sustainability is *strategic*: when you incorporate it into your core values, you can create competitive advantage. And the way to do that is to pursue sustainability as you would any other strategic initiative. Now that you have this mindset, let's briefly explore some other approaches to improving resilience through sustainability.

First, one productive way to think about sustainability is *reducing waste*. Nobody likes waste. Now your waste reduction efforts can both improve your bottom line and improve the planet. Furthermore, the scale of the problem coincides with your new, resilience-based interest in collaborating across the supply chain. How can you collaborate with suppliers to reduce even more waste?

Some companies gain benefits here from a *digital twin*, which is a digital replica of a physical asset or real-world process—an airplane, an office building, a factory, or a supply chain. In mimicking a supply chain's assets, steps, transactions, relationships, and other working details, the twin permits you to do advanced, real-time monitoring and testing of future scenarios. It's great for supply chains in general—DHL has one for warehousing— but it can be especially valuable in looking at sustainability.[12]

Second, another productive way to think about sustainability is in terms of *design*. There used to be a perceived trade-off between *sustainable* design and *economical or profitable* design. But sustainability is no longer niche. For example, from 2015–2020, nearly 50% of consumer goods' growth was driven by sustainably marketed products. In a 2022 survey, 99% of respondents said they were taking actions that they believed were helping the environment. So one place to drive sustainability into your company's strategy and values is in your design thinking.[13]

And again, *sustainability* here refers to much more than carbon reduction. Many clients of Kearney's Product Excellence and Renewal Lab (PERLab) are thinking about sustainability in terms of worker safety, ergonomics training, and other social components of their ESG agendas. Just as *sustainable design* becomes simply *design*, so too do *employee-centric, socially conscious, community replenishing*, and other value-based approaches to design.

A third productive way to think about sustainability is in terms of diversity. As any farmer can tell you, homogeneity breeds vulnerability. Or any banana eater. Until the 1950s, almost all globally exported bananas were thick-peeled, densely bunched Gros Michel varieties. But a disease wiped out vast populations, and now we all eat blander Cavendish bananas. Might a smart banana grower use a diversity of cultivars? And might a smart company similarly rely on a diversity of employees and suppliers? People with different backgrounds allow for creative problem-solving.

Fourth, a final productive way to think about sustainability is as a step toward circular business models. In the *circular economy*, all end-of-life materials are used as input for new product cycles. This eliminates waste and emissions and ensures the safe and responsible use of the world's natural resources. Complete societal circularity, if it's even possible, is obviously decades away. But the world doesn't have to achieve the entire vision for some of its tenets to be useful.

After all, the linear nature of existing supply chains promotes extraction of virgin resources followed by disposal of used products. As resources become more scarce and environmental degradation becomes a greater concern, *reuse* becomes a lot more desirable—a lot more profitable. Furthermore, an imperative to become more circular may soon arise from regulations, especially in Europe. Or the imperative may arise from internal strategy and values. A Kearney survey found that companies that have taken the lead in implementing and integrating circular initiatives into their operations reap monetary and reputational benefits.

Circularity may involve a radical shift in business models or even a rethinking of value creation. Maybe you emphasize access over ownership, or performance over new products. (See the sidebar, "Case Example: Achieving Circularity Through New Partnerships and Technologies.") This is heady, long-term stuff. You shouldn't try it overnight. But thinking about it and asking these questions is a way of embarking on a corporate journey. That journey's first destination may be sustainability. But its final goal is resilience.[14]

---

**CASE EXAMPLE: ACHIEVING CIRCULARITY THROUGH NEW PARTNERSHIPS AND TECHNOLOGIES**

Inspired by the 2015 Paris Accords, a technology company announced its intention to reach net-zero carbon emissions by 2040. It then doubled down on the science to show the sincerity of the pledge: it would follow the Science-Based Targets initiative (SBTi); it would address emissions in scopes 1, 2, and 3; it would simultaneously address supplier diversity; and it would commit to transforming its operations to shrink emissions as much as possible, rather than simply buying carbon offsets.

*(continued)*

*(continued)*

How would it translate these 2040 targets into actionable initiatives? The first step was to establish a baseline. Working with heuristics and assumptions, the company established a rough estimate of the sources of these emissions. Similar to most tech companies, it found greatest emissions in scope 3. When customers used its products, they consumed electricity. Suppliers also generated far more emissions than the company did itself.

Based on this baseline, the firm was able to define actionable targets on a functional level—for procurement, R&D, sales, and other functions. The targets corresponded to each function's contribution to overall emissions. Then the company put all the targets on a road map that defined clear milestones. It cited the proverb about eating the elephant one bite at a time. And because different units and functions were responsible for fulfilling those plans, no one person has to eat an entire elephant.

The company was aware of the German Supply Chain Act (Lieferkettensorgfaltspflichtengesetz, or LkSG) and a looming supply chain act from the European Union. It did plenty of business in Germany, so it needed to gain transparency into its supply base. The good news: the company already had in place a standard code of conducts and audits. The bad news: it had no transparency into tier 2 suppliers, much less beyond them—and LkSG would clearly require that transparency.

Working with its most strategic suppliers, the company mapped its tier 2 supply. It scored those tier 2 suppliers on ESG risks, most notably environmental impacts and labor/human rights. This was a relatively "manual" process, without external data providers or advanced analytics. The company was simply having an open dialogue with suppliers. As a result, it was able to build a database and risk scorecard for all of its tier 2 suppliers.

Meanwhile, the company addressed internal sources of carbon emissions. Because these were under its control, the timeline to achieve reduction objectives was much shorter—2025 or 2030 in most cases. At the measurement step, it had installed a network of thousands of physical and virtual sensors looking at how its factories used electricity, fossil fuels, water, and other energy and environmental inputs. Now it could benchmark energy efficiency across sites and technologies. It linked and consolidated data to continually identify new efficiency opportunities. After all, these delivered not only environmental benefits but also cost savings.

Another early victory came in reducing plastic packaging. The company launched a series of cross-functional workshops with marketing, sales, procurement, packaging engineers, and suppliers. The workshops identified multiple options for reducing packaging waste:

- For some products, the company moved from plastic to paper packaging at a similar cost—and a strong sustainability marketing effect.
- For other products, it changed the shape and thickness of the plastic packaging, resulting in 30% less material required. This also translated into significant material cost savings.
- Where neither option was viable, the company found other ways to reduce waste in its processes. For example, it could adjust machinery to reduce how much "forerun" a roll of plastic film would need. It could change printing technology, reducing the number of colors used. And it could improve pallet utilization to reduce emissions (and costs) of transportation.

The initiative led to a significant decrease in consumer waste. It also resulted in approximately 10% cost savings on the company's total packaging spend. Finally, it fostered internal cross-functional cooperation and sparked ideas for further collaboration with suppliers.

Not all of its initiatives panned out. But sometimes it took a flier on an unlikely seeming angle. For example, one of its product lines generated a lot of scrap metal. So it explored a partnership with a new type of waste management service provider. This provider didn't want a fixed sum per ton of waste handled. Instead, it worked together with the company and other clients to find other industries that wanted their waste products. Some of this company's scrap metal had just the right composition needed by a manufacturer of specific alloys. The waste-using manufacturer was also a client of this unique service provider. So the company developed a new revenue stream, selling its waste. The waste-using manufacturer saved money on its supplies. And the service provider took a cut, for its role in creating the market and organizing the logistics.

Is it confusing or overwhelming to have so many balls in the air? Sure, at times. But the company understands that different initiatives have different complexities, different times to completion. And they're all needed: climate change won't be addressed by a single silver bullet. For the company, the best part is that it is improving—internally and externally—a general mindset around sustainability. If it can build momentum, the future challenges will be easier to solve.

# CHAPTER 7

# Fit the Principles to Your Situation and Strategy

In each of the preceding five chapters (Chapters 2–6), we've started with some basic ideas (*Listen to customers! Reduce carbon!*). And we've gradually moved into ideas that would require pretty big corporate transformations (*Put "constant learning" at the core of your values?! Emphasize access over ownership?!?!?*). That's not because we expect every reader of this book to run with all of these ideas. Rather, it's because in our experience the companies that do execute successful transformations are on a journey that's shaped a lot like this.

*But I don't want to transform*, you may be saying. *I just want to become a little more resilient!* That's fine. In Part II, we'll provide you with plenty of details on how to implement specific resilience practices, and with concrete examples of companies strengthening their supply chains. We believe you will be better at implementing those projects now that you have read Part I and understand the bigger picture. You'll see how the five principles support each other, for example, how an effort to qualify backup suppliers can be enriched by thinking about customer preferences or data analytics.

To close with just one more story: A global metallurgy player acquired a major Asia-based competitor. It saw opportunities to increase efficiency, optimize its carbon footprint, and become more resilient in the supplier dimension. So as part of its post-merger integration activities, it took a close look at core functions such as procurement, operations, supply chain, transportation, and logistics, as well as marketing and sales. And it discovered resilience opportunities in technology. It developed an AI-based engine to optimize raw materials, improve plant footprints, efficiently allocate its hundreds of customers and 110,000 products across 25 global plants, and lower its carbon footprint. This tool, now embedded in its software and in its sales and operations planning (S&OP) processes, has already improved EBITDA by more than €10 million. In addition, the company identified supplier/raw material/ formulation combinations that were highly exposed to supply disruptions, finding ways to increase resilience. Did this company intend to set out on a transformation journey? Or did it pursue some basic ideas and gradually embark on a larger, more productive transformation?

While you're pondering that question, we'd like to suggest a few more—of a more provocative variety—to help take the lessons of this chapter home with you. (See the sidebar, "Some Provocative Questions.")

You'll pick and choose among the principles, fitting them to your situation—knowing that they interact. Talent enables digital; technology enhances talent. Sustainability enables talent; talent drives sustainability. The supply base will affect customer base; the customer base should drive the supply base. You'll need that knowledge as you combat others' temptations to think in silos. You'll know that siloed thinking won't achieve resilience. After all, the whole point of resilience is to spread the risk rather than concentrating it.

At the same time, however, we believe that your first steps toward resilience will prove to be your first steps on a long journey. True resilience will require transformation. Even if you don't believe that now, you may believe it after your first project. Or your second. Or your fourth. Or maybe you'll never believe it, until years from now when you look back at what your company was, and who you were, when you first read this book, and you think, "Huh, looks like we transformed." (Will your next thought be, "Might have been easier if we hadn't resisted it"?)

## SOME PROVOCATIVE QUESTIONS

As you seek to apply these principles at your own company, you'll use specific actions similar to those we describe in Part II. But to explore their implications, and to motivate your team, you may want to think about the principles in terms of questions like these:

- (Suppliers) What would your balance sheet look like if you needed to write off all assets in noncore markets? Would your company still exist? This could happen in a major geopolitical conflict. Indeed, many firms had to ask themselves this question, albeit at a smaller scale, in recent conflicts. On a bigger scale, similar happenings could have significant cashflow and balance sheet implications. And apart from the accounting issues, many supply chains would simply break down. Even if you'd be fine, your suppliers might not be. How would that play out?
- (Suppliers) How many tier 2 and tier 3 suppliers do you have? Who are they? Have you ever spoken to a single one? If you lack visibility into tier 2 and beyond, you will struggle to prepare for upstream disruptions. And why haven't you talked to these suppliers? Do you think their inputs are less crucial to your product than the inputs from your tier 1 supplier? Or do you trust that your tier 1 supplier is better at supplier relationship management than you are?
- (Customers) What percentage of your revenue is clustered in a specific geography? Could you remove this customer cluster without becoming insolvent? A trade war's import quotas or retaliatory tariffs could lose you an entire country or region. What would that do to your margins? Your asset utilization numbers shrink, your fixed costs are spread across fewer sales—are you still okay? Can you repurpose and pivot to sell something else to someone else? Or are you stuck with assets and distribution networks that are geared toward a market you can no longer serve?
- (Employees) Do you have the right incentives in place to excite the next generation of talents? Your resilience and strength come from your people. And your people are increasingly motivated by purpose and joy, rather than simple monetary bonuses. Can you satisfy them?
- (Technology) What is the next big technological disruption in your sector? Will it center on improved visibility, collaborative automation, or constant learning? Each could have profound impacts on

*(continued)*

(*continued*)

your business model—but the first step is to understand the coming changes. Are you actively looking for them?

- (Sustainability) If you were no longer allowed any single-use, non-recyclable materials, would your business still exist? A less-drastic version of this situation might become a reality. Regulations and consumer demands will gradually make some materials unusable. This includes regulations on your suppliers—they may decide to exit a market rather than invest in the transformations needed to make your input more environmentally friendly. If that happens, do you have options ready to use? How would those options affect your operations? How would they transform your supply base?

- (Sustainability) What would your annual bonus look like if it was tied to reaching sustainability targets? Here's one example: imagine that reaching only 50% of your emission targets cuts your bonus in half (and reaching none of the targets cuts your bonus to zero). Another example: imagine that your bonus is reduced by a factor corresponding to every percentage point of employee turnover in your department. Would you still get a bonus? Do you now owe your company money? Why is that? And what if these two examples were combined? Is sustainability performance related to employee retention? We know that it's difficult to make high profits (thus ensuring your bonus) while also being environmentally friendly and treating your employees well. But we believe it's even more difficult to sustain performance over more than two to three years if you're not ticking all three boxes.

Every transformation is unique. There's no one–size–fits–all approach. But we would like to suggest that some combination of these five principles will be—should be—at the core of how you transform. You will define how the principles fit into your current strategy. You will identify the ones that will boost you the most. Then you will combine them, perhaps gaining synergies.

Transformation can feel daunting. But for daunting experiences, how about a global pandemic? Your company survived that. You might have discovered inner strengths, and/or you might have decided that things couldn't go on the way they had been. You needed a change, a transformation. That impulse was correct.

But don't just change *away* from something. Away from continual crises or employee burnout or a lost sense of joy. Change *toward* something. Embrace an opportunity. In this new VUCA world, some firms will have the resilience to thrive. We'll be blunt: yours probably isn't one of them—now. But it could be. Easily. Whatever your strengths, you can build on them to enrich your resilience and drive those values into your core. Your transformation begins with the first steps toward strengthening your supply chain for resilient operations.

PART II

# From Strategy to Action: Implementing the Five Principles

It's easy to have opinions. Many people can spout opinions about sports, politics, and even the best paths to building strong supply chains for resilient operations (although, granted, maybe this last one is a smaller subset of people). What's hard, and thus what distinguishes a leader, is the ability to execute: to throw a touchdown pass, or craft effective legislation, or implement an operations project. That's why we're devoting the biggest section of this book to implementation. Here we'll show you how to put these principles into action.

Each of the next five chapters is devoted to the principles discussed in Part I: how to improve resilience through suppliers, customers, employees, technology, and sustainability, respectively. Each chapter features five approaches—projects that you can implement at various levels of your organization. Each approach features one or more examples to inspire you with the details of how someone else did it.

Obviously you won't implement all of these projects. Some of them are industry-specific. Some are historical, to demonstrate the permanence of this wisdom rather than the way things work today. Some of the approaches are more tactical, perhaps best executed by a team lead or local manager. And other approaches are more strategic, perhaps best driven by a vice president or head of a business unit. (Within each chapter, the approaches generally broaden from the more tactical to the more strategic.) This mix is by design: we believe that people at all levels of a firm can benefit from understanding these approaches. Also, recall that one key to resilience is avoiding silos, so even if you are not driving one of these projects, you may need to support it. Such support is always easier when buttressed by understanding.

As we discussed in Chapter 7, we believe these projects can and should be part of a broader corporate transformation (a theme we'll return to in Part III). But, as Chapter 7 also discusses, the transformation part is what schoolteachers used to call *extra credit*. If you want to pick just a few of these projects—the ones that best resonate with your firm's philosophy and organization—that's great. Your resilience will improve. And this is certainly not an exhaustive list of what can be done. Indeed, if you do embark on a transformation, you will surely execute projects not mentioned here, because you are moving beyond the scope of what a book like this can cover.

But we expect that these approaches can do a few things for you:

- Ground the five principles in details of their implementation.
- Highlight the actions that can drive the spirit of the transformation according to the five principles.
- Show how the five principles and their implementation overlap—and thus show how change doesn't happen in isolation, but needs to be a holistic, firm-wide process.

But enough with our opinions of what Part II can do for you! Let's march forward to implement these ideas.

CHAPTER 8

# Build Resilience Against Supply Shocks by Working with Supplier Ecosystems

Recent events have demonstrated the need for strong, resilient supply chains. But you can't just conjure them out of thin air. You need to transform your relationships with existing and new suppliers. Here are five ways to make that happen.

## Turn Your Supply Chain into a Network by Developing Second Sources and Qualifying Backup Suppliers

Risks arise in your supply chain when you have a single source. If that source becomes unavailable, you're stuck—even if the item being supplied is relatively minor or substitutable. So to reduce risks, you want to reduce your single-source dependencies.

This may feel counterintuitive. Under the lean philosophy, you wanted to find one incredibly efficient supplier and then maximize economies of scale. With increasing pressure on time to market, that instinct only grows. Who else could do this? But sometimes, dependency on a single supplier results from ossified bureaucracy. Have you taken approaches to make your products more "sourceable"? For example, you want to specify it as little as possible, explore increased tolerances, and otherwise give other suppliers a fair shake. Kearney research shows that two out of three supplier monopolies in engineering-driven companies are customer caused. They focus on *best technical solution* and *first to market* due to ownership by engineering and sales. If you instead take a *design for sourcing* approach, you optimize product design and engineering choices to achieve best total cost of ownership across your supplier value chain.[1]

Let's say you're doing this work for Coyote Enterprises. First, map your current spend. Your procurement organization should be familiar with the process of building a spend cube. Indeed, ideally the process is automated, perhaps using a dedicated software package and/or AI to make updates. This analysis will show you that all of the critical products in your Roadrunner initiative come from the Acme Corporation.[2]

So review the product history: Have the products arrived on time? Have they performed as advertised? Do they fit well into your corporate culture, or is there too much room for user error? Now look at the contracts. Why *is* this single sourced? Is there an intellectual property issue? Did your predecessor make a lengthy commitment?

Now you can screen the market for alternatives. Depending on your situation, we suggest using one or more of the following approaches:

- Perform desktop research.
- Buy market reports.
- Work with dedicated supplier scouting firms, such as Scoutbee, Tealbook, Ariba Discovery, or Alpas.
- Work with a consultancy that has a track record in the specific industries you're targeting.
- Discuss with industry peers and/or industry associations.

When you get some ideas, conduct a request for information/proposal (RFI/RFP). This process will help you better understand the suppliers' capabilities and also ensure that their pricing is at least within the range of what you had in mind. Meanwhile, talk to R&D and manufacturing to fully understand your needs, requirements, and internal capacities. Ensure to block some of that capacity!

Then you can invite promising suppliers to sit down and talk with you. What can they do for you? What is their pricing? And, critically, you need to figure out the risks associated with these alternatives. For example, if they're in the same country as your original supplier—or rely on inputs from the same country—you may face similar geopolitical and transport risks. They may not be a desirable backup. But don't get discouraged. You're never going to eliminate *all* risk. Instead your goal is to diversify the risks, such that any one crisis doesn't shut you down.

When you find valid suppliers, start to qualify the most competitive ones as second sources or backups. If you lose a single supplier, either partially or fully, you now have a fallback plan. Indeed, if necessary, you can also use the alternative source to cover peaks. Or if your incumbent supplier increases prices, you can shift volumes. Even if none of these situations come to pass, you can be secure in the knowledge that your supply chain no longer has a weak link—it has an alternative.

Of course there are pitfalls. As noted, if your backup is in the same geography as your incumbent, or uses the same tier 2 supplier, you're not reducing much risk. Yet on the flip side, if you qualify too many backups, you're driving up cost and complexity. This is a balancing act: cost versus risk. Too few sources, and your risk is too high. Too many sources, and you lose economies of scale or valuable partnerships. This is why you mapped your spend and identified the inputs that most required diversification. It's also why you need transparency beyond your tier 1 suppliers. You are seeking to tailor your supply base for specific inputs based on what each input needs more: resilience or efficiency.

You also need to manage the relationship with your backup suppliers. They need transparency as to how much volume they can expect. If you promise more than you deliver—if you suggest that they will win the entire volume of a $10 million RFP, but then only give them 10% of that—then the effort you put into building the relationship may go to waste. It's fine to give them 10% as long as that's clearly communicated. Indeed, you might find it be valuable to give regular smaller volumes to your backups so that they are getting benefits from the relationship. This also ensures that they retain the ability to manufacture according to your specifications, because those specs may change more rapidly than you expect.[3]

## Do Not Only Focus on Cost, but Optimize Collaboratively with Your Supplier

When you used the lean philosophy, your systems were completely organized around costs. All of your suppliers' incentives were to produce as cheap as possible. And all of your employees' incentives were to negotiate on price. Now that we have a better understanding of risks (and now that the risks seem to be proliferating) you need to instead seek value.

Thus, as you talk to a supplier, share information. *Here's what we want to achieve. How can you help us?* After all, the supplier wants to help you—that will lead to more business for them. When you explain what will make you successful, that may spur the supplier to generate additional good ideas.

Those good ideas will go beyond prices. Low prices are still great—but you may also be able to find mutual advantages by exploring joint optimization levers on process, logistics, design, or other elements of your relationship.

This means your procurement people must understand what will make you successful. In the past, all they had to know was market prices, because that was all they would negotiate on. Now they need a bigger picture: both why and how this input contributes to customer value. They also need to be empowered, with R&D and manufacturing willing to participate in the broader negotiations.

No doubt, that internal alignment can be difficult. For example, success at collaborative optimization may require design changes. R&D and engineering have to align on these changes. Sometimes people are reluctant to endorse changes that aren't their idea. So you need to involve them early. And because you're changing processes, you have to carefully delineate ownership and road maps. Who is in charge of these negotiations? Who implements the optimizations? When should the various actions be taking place? Your previous, cost-focused negotiations had a clear road map based on decades of experience. Now you have different priorities and processes—but that doesn't mean you should operate without any road map at all.

External alignment can be problematic as well. You should begin this process only with *key* suppliers—incumbents with a big spend. You're not doing this for, say, office supplies. And you want to make sure the supplier is sincere. Some suppliers will try to offer you a "reward in heaven"—a great deal that is either difficult to quantify or not tied to a clear road map. For example, when talk comes to action, they apologize that they can't deliver on the promised 10% discount because the design change needs more testing; it'll be available next year. Or maybe they make unwarranted assumptions about your cost savings, claiming that higher-stacked pallets will save you 20% in the cost of storage space (well, only if you can reduce your warehouse size by 20%), or that 10% fewer shipments will save you 10% in process costs (well, only if you reduce warehouse headcount by 10%). Such tricks often suggest that they are not negotiating in good faith. Suppliers that are worthy of partnerships will agree to quantifiable, tangible targets. They will work with you to set a baseline and then contractually define year-on-year improvements against this baseline.

How do you find the opportunities and targets? You could just *ask for ideas*. That may sound overly simple. But you may be surprised at how many ideas your suppliers have. They've always had ideas. You just used to stop listening to them after they gave you a price. Obviously you need to evaluate ideas internally in a structured, cross-functional process. Are they feasible? Would they contribute value? How excited are the stakeholders?

Another valuable approach is to include an *off-specification* section in new RFPs for your category. The typical RFP asks potential new suppliers to give you a quote based on your specifications—but what if they could change those specs? In this section, they could say, *If I could change this material . . .* or *If I could deliver a full truck monthly instead of a half truck twice a month. . . .* Here is a source of great ideas for collaborative optimization. If you have sufficient storage space, then the full truck monthly cuts unneeded logistics costs. If an alternate material is more plentiful in a different geographic region, then it's providing an opportunity to mitigate geopolitical risks. Discuss these ideas internally and with the suppliers. Depending on relationships, you could even discuss a challenger's alternate ideas with your incumbent suppliers! (See the sidebar, "Deliver 9 to 5?")

---

### DELIVER 9 TO 5?

An online retailer of medical equipment was spending too much for its express home deliveries to end consumers. Inflation was putting pressure on its margins, but given the capacity crunch in the logistics market, its incumbent provider was unwilling to make concessions on price. So it issued an RFP.

By standard measures, the RFP failed. All of the challengers quoted prices significantly **higher** than the incumbent. But the company had included an off-specification section. Multiple challengers provided off-specification bids that could be up to 30% cheaper than the incumbent. The catch was that the company had to relax its specified time delivery window of 9:00 a.m. to 5:00 p.m.

The company discussed the idea internally. Why did the window exist? Wouldn't abolishing the window actually **improve** customer value? People were typically out of the house between 9:00 and 5:00—they'd rather get their deliveries before or after work. It turned out that the time delivery window had been established by the incumbent supplier. The supplier had subtly planted within the company a set of pointless specs that its competitors would struggle to meet.

Empowered by this analysis, the company switched to a new supplier that offered significantly better rates and better service quality. The switch saved the company 20% on its total parcel logistics spend.

When you and your supplier only ever negotiated on price, your relationship was strictly transactional. Your continued demands for lower prices threatened their margins and pressured them to cut costs without sacrificing quality. When you optimize collaboratively, you have a stronger relationship. And resilience is all about relationships.

If your suppliers can see you as a partner, rather than a demanding taskmaster, they will be more likely to support you when you're in trouble. When you let them see your goals and processes, you extend your creative networks. You also model behavior that, if they follow it, will enable you to better understand your suppliers and their vulnerabilities. Those vulnerabilities—we all have them—are sources of risk. Resilience means knowing what they are ahead of time, rather than being surprised by them amid the crisis.

## Enter Strategic Partnerships and Invest in Your Suppliers' Fitness to Ensure You Have the Right Partners at the Right Time

At the beginning of the 20th century, entrepreneur Harry Child ran a string of hotels in Yellowstone National Park. Before widespread automobile travel, all of Child's guests arrived by train. That meant he had a very close partnership with the Northern Pacific Railroad (NPRR).

Because NPRR valued the partnership, it gave Child all sorts of things. A loan, without the hassles of an external bank? Help negotiating with his suppliers? Lobbying of government regulators? To Child, it almost felt as if the railroad was working for him. Yet to NPRR, the help cemented the relationship. The railroad saw Child as a smart businessman with a deep understanding of his industry, his local conditions, and NPRR's own needs. Their partnership was a win-win.[4]

In the previous section ("Do Not Only Focus on Cost, but Optimize Collaboratively with Your Supplier") we used the term *partnership* loosely: you want a *spirit* of partnership with your suppliers. But in some cases you should go ahead and formalize the strategic partnership. Maybe you even invest in your suppliers. The goal is to make sure that these smart, talented people will continue to provide you with a win-win.

As a first step, invite your key suppliers to come visit so that you can get to know them. Then send your people to the supplier's site. And not just procurement people, but engineers, quality experts, and executives. You should arrange for a meeting between your chief procurement officer and the supplier's CEO—or even a CEO-CEO summit.

Over time, these meetings should establish trust. If and when that happens, start to open your books. Note that we're not talking about financing or cost calculation methods. We're talking about an open, trusting exploration. You explore their processes, they explore yours. Together, you find ways to jointly optimize. For example, on one of your site visits, your engineers may identify inefficiencies. Then you and the supplier can jointly design solutions to alleviate them. Maybe it's more efficient for the supplier to adjust its shipping procedures—or for you to adjust your receiving procedures.

Collaborative optimization is always a partnership. As you work with suppliers, you will come to better understand them and their pain points. You need to build trust by honoring agreements and jointly improving your partnership. You must not abuse this trust. Your inspection of your supplier's production line can never end with you dictating terms. Perhaps you will think, "Boy, investing in improvements here and there will allow you to reduce costs by 10%!" But you can't demand that they reduce prices by 10%. You can expect it, you can discuss it, you can debate who gets what share of the expected benefits. But you can't dictate outcomes.

A cautionary tale: We know of one company that sent its engineers to spend a week at the plant of a cooperative supplier. They combed up and down the factory and learned how the supplier did everything. A year after the engineers got home, the company announced that it would insource production, cutting out the supplier entirely. After all, they'd learned everything, right? Then they realized that there was one particular part that they couldn't make at the required quality, and the supplier could. "Hey, would you guys be interested . . . ?" It was a quick conversation to kick off a long, painful journey: the once-cooperative supplier hung up.

At the same time, you do have to look out for yourself. Even as you develop the strategic partnership, you should still have a backup ready just in case. And you shouldn't beat a dead horse. Some small suppliers may deserve financial help such as bank guarantees. But if your supplier will clearly fail—because of high debt, old technology, or a lack of other viable customers—then your past work with that supplier represents sunk costs. You need to look for a different supplier. If you keep this one on life support, you're just setting up a situation in which they will end up blackmailing you. This sort of dependence is actually making you *less* resilient.

And the goal, of course, is more resilience. When you ensure your key suppliers' fitness, you reduce the risk that these suppliers will fail you in a time of need. Or at worst, the strengthened relationship and transparency will help you tell much earlier if something is amiss. You are strengthening potentially weak links in your supply chain, creating an empowered ecosystem. This is the kind of supply chain that can bend but not break in crises.

## Extend Your Supplier Management to Tier 2—and Beyond—by Helping Your Suppliers Develop Their Suppliers

In the past, sometimes the success of the lean supply chain depended on an *out-of-sight, out-of-mind* illusion. If you could move risks to your suppliers, your bottom line would look better. Your suppliers thought the same way. Potential labor problems or geopolitical tensions or logistics snafus might imperil that other company, but not *us*.

For decades, few such risks materialized, making belief in the illusion seem smart. But now we've seen some of the risks materialize. For example, some automakers had basically handed all of their supply management functions to their tier 1 suppliers. If something went wrong, they had a scapegoat ready. But in the semiconductor crisis, the problem was rooted in tier 3 and beyond. No tier 1 supplier was prepared. And the automakers themselves were not only unprepared, but completely unaware.

In short, we've discovered that you can still be imperiled by risks on other companies' balance sheets. You need to account for all of the risks in the ecosystem.

It's not enough to manage your suppliers. You need to extend your supplier management to your suppliers' suppliers—and maybe even beyond. Indeed, new regulations such as the German Supply Chain Due Diligence Act (Lieferkettensorgfaltspflichtengesetz, or LkSG) will require it.[5] The regulations are looking for transparency: you need to *know* whether any company in your supply chain is abusing people or the environment. But as you develop transparency, you might as well develop relationships too. Your suppliers need healthy relationships with their suppliers—and you can help. For example, you can add your weight and expertise to their supplier negotiations. You can help them extend supplier fitness programs to their supply base. Or you can help them map their supply base and identify alternative sources of supply.

The easiest way to start an initiative like this is to let it grow out of the previous initiatives in this section. You've identified key suppliers. You're building trust with them. As part of that trust, you're being transparent about your goals and any regulatory hurdles you face. So now you ask if they would be willing to share information about their supply base. And you invest in the technology to compile this information into databases that help you map your value chain.

Again, in a trusting relationship, this can be a constructive two-way street. You can ask your suppliers if they need help with, say, negotiations. Indeed these topics might come up naturally. Your supplier reaches out with a price increase ("We need to increase prices by 4% because our raw material supplier has increased their prices by 10%, and 40% of our cost structure is material cost."). You respond, "Hey, I'm glad you brought this up. Are these interchangeable components, or critical ones?"

As you do get to know your tier 2 suppliers, explore where you can use your weight to help them. Your goal is to help empower the ecosystem. If your suppliers' suppliers could benefit from logistics adjustments or government lobbying or consumer awareness, you may have the capabilities to boost yourself by boosting them.

The biggest pitfall in this process may be the temptation to drift from *managing* your suppliers to thinking of them as an *extension of your firm*. First of all, when you think that way, you're being patronizing. That's a surefire way to alienate suppliers. You need to always acknowledge that they are their own entities. Second, they might be also working for your competitors. Certainly the farther upstream you get—tier 2, tier 3—the more likely that is. And that's fine: you're taking advantage of their scale, while you and your tier 1 suppliers add the unique features that give you competitive advantage. But it reinforces that they are not extensions of your firm; you need to manage them with respect for their autonomy.

Another potential pitfall concerns efforts to gain transparency through external data service providers. These are companies that will sell you data on, say, emissions of a textile factory in Dhaka or the labor practices of a factory in Shenzhen. These data providers can be helpful. But you cannot rely 100% on the data. Most of these companies don't conduct audits themselves. They collect reports from governmental and other auditors. In countries with weak institutions, these audits may not be trustworthy. Seeing is believing: it's always better to engage with your suppliers and double-check everything.

Yet at the same time you can't get lost in complexity. If you have 1,000 suppliers and each of them has 1,000 suppliers, then your tier 2 network could be as many as 1 million suppliers! That's too much data to track. Focus where you can make a difference.

Making a difference: as we argued in Chapter 6, you should think of sustainability issues as not political but strategic. It's not about *obeying regulations*, it's about developing strengths. Extending your supplier management will provide you with valuable transparency into your tier 2 and tier 3 networks. This transparency will give you early knowledge of disruptions.

Assuming you do the supplier relationship management correctly, you are also gaining understanding of potential risks. That gives you more agency to mitigate them. For example, you may see geographic clustering and geopolitical risks that you might not have been aware of. Also, sustainability risks—such as suppliers with unethical working conditions—aren't just about regulation. In your spectrum of fears, getting fined should rank pretty low. Far bigger: having a supplier forced to shut down because of ESG violations such as child labor or environmental pollution. Or worst of all: having media coverage and activist campaigns turn customers against you. These are risks definitely worth mitigating.

# Source "in the Region, for the Region" through Re- and Nearshoring

As this book has continually argued, your reshoring decisions should be part of a broader discussion about resilience and operations transformation. We are fans of reshoring. But not because it's trendy. That's why we like to use the phrase "in the region, for the region." In some industries, creating multiple regional nodes of operation—where supply, manufacturing, and sales are linked—is the most resilient and profitable setup.

To bring essential parts of your supply base closer to your operations, you have two choices. One is to offer incentives to your existing suppliers to move their manufacturing sites closer to yours. This is obviously an action you take with a trusted partner. Based on your past relations with the supplier, you know that it will respond well to the incentives; the reshoring effort is a joint journey.

The second approach is to switch to local suppliers. Again, it's a partnership. You may need to help them build their capacities in both the literal and figurative senses. Literal: they may need to increase production to meet your increased demand, and to do so, they may want up-front guarantees, long-term commitments, and/or even financial help. Figurative: you may be able to aid them in their supplier relations or some of the other topics just discussed.

Start with a long-term scenario analysis of your supply base. What happens to your supply chain under different macroeconomic, geopolitical, and logistics scenarios? For example, a global recession, a long-term increase in energy prices, a regional political shift away from free-trade principles, a war, an increase in natural disasters—how would your global suppliers be affected?

Meanwhile, consider the domestic manufacturing ecosystem. This includes upcoming regulations, environmental or safety concerns, subsidies for reshoring, and other political factors. Do you have domestic capacity—does the expertise exist to perform this work? Or can you easily create it? And how about nearshoring options? Can you use nearby countries? What are the benefits and risks?

These analyses will help you identify potential reshoring inputs. Now you can develop a long-term business case. Then you can start conversations with your suppliers about how to make it happen. By the way, depending on your industry and size, you may want to explore joining forces with competitors to get the critical mass of demand that would entice suppliers to make the necessary investments. You may invest in suppliers or explore joint ventures. Given the political popularity of reshoring, regulators are unlikely to complain about anticompetitive aspects of such collaborations. Instead, the hurdle you may face is that so many industries lack an effective industry association or buying consortium to provide the needed communication channels.

Reshoring has costs. You need to understand those costs up front so that you can make intelligent decisions about the trade-offs involved. For example, reshoring will likely reduce your economies of scale. It will increase your labor costs (that's why you offshored to begin with). It may also require you to commit time and/or money to your suppliers. How will you absorb these cost increases?

As you weigh pluses and minuses, be sure that your reshoring effort is effectively addressing the problem. If you merely reshore the closest link, but those suppliers are still getting 100% of their inputs from the globalized supply chain, you haven't really strengthened your supply chain. You've merely reduced your own visibility into potential problems.

Finally, if you're a major player, reshoring may expose you to retaliation. For example, if you pull all of your manufacturing capacity out of a specific country, but you also sell in that country, might it limit your access to its domestic demand market? Reshoring discussions, especially in the abstract, can be oddly focused on developed countries. Granted, those are the countries that outsourced to begin with. But the world has changed. Now you can apply the "in the region, for the region" lens to *any* geographic region, as we see in Chapter 9.

Although all of these are ways that companies can fumble reshoring efforts, they remain attractive, and rightly so. The biggest benefit of reshoring comes in the reduction of long transport ways. Indeed, sometimes you can even eliminate them. By removing your dependence on sea and air transport, you greatly reduce infrastructure risk, such as delays caused by congested ports, terrorism, or bad weather. You also greatly reduce lead times, which makes you much more flexible.

Reshoring also frees you from import quotas. It's much easier to comply with local content regulations. In some highly regulated industries you can increase agility when you don't cross international borders. And in some cases, such as semiconductors, you may be helping to fulfill a local government's industrial policy. Finally, to the extent that your local customers value local production (or may come to value it in the future), you are building resilience in the customer dimension as well.

# CHAPTER 9

# Build Resilience Against Demand Shocks by Operating for the Customer

Genuine resilience requires not only rethinking relationships with suppliers but also extending your analysis all the way to your customers. Here are five ways to build resilience against changes in customer demand.

## Listen to Your Customer Through Customer Sharing Sessions and Automated Feedback

"*At the end of this book, please turn the final page to answer a brief two-question survey.*" You'd do it, wouldn't you? Only two questions, after you've invested so much time in this book? After you've enjoyed it so much? (You *are* enjoying it, aren't you? You've already read about half of it!!) Sadly, we can't implement such a survey because the technology of the old-fashioned book doesn't allow it.

But we *should* care about what you think. (And we do! How about this: email us at ResilientOperationsBook@kearney.com.) Listening to customers is the world's oldest path to business success. And in contrast to books (which have other strengths), many of today's technologies make it easy.

All companies claim to know what their customers want. All claim to listen to their customer base. But many of them are just paying lip service. Either they don't collect feedback or they don't act on the feedback that they do receive. To stand out from the pack, you can have regular customer sharing sessions. Or you can find ways to generate feedback in a more automated manner.

Do your customers have a regular opportunity to share their views? Do you actively encourage them to do so? Map your customers' journey. At what point(s) do they interact with you? What is the most appropriate time to engage them and ask for feedback? For example, you could reach out a few weeks after purchase. It's tricky to find the right time. Not immediately, but not too long after—and ideally at a time when the customer has nothing better to do. Some companies take advantage of the moment when customers buy a refill or accessories, although that moment introduces bias by not reaching customers who were dissatisfied enough to walk away without refilling or accessorizing.

Now decide *how* to engage them. Craft your questions in ways that will bring meaningful answers. When those answers arrive, study them: What are the common themes? Are there patterns, for example in demographics, regions, or use cases? What can you learn from them? What do they mean for your product and your operations?

This may become a core competency. In the beauty industry, for instance, startup brands such as ColourPop, Kylie, Tata Harper, Tula, and ScentBird all challenged established industry players by focusing on designing new products and experiences and creating deep consumer intimacy. They relied on third parties for everything else—manufacturing, online shopping platforms, and direct-to-consumer delivery.[1]

There are certainly rules to think about. You are trying to enhance your customer relationships by soliciting information that you will process and take action on. That means:

- Don't overdo it with the feedback requests. You don't want to annoy the customer.
- A popup where they enter 1 to 5 stars is not sufficiently meaningful. You want to ask for constructive improvements.
- Your goal is to *listen* to consumers, not *educate* them. If they are not using the product the way you intended, that is valuable input to your design, product development, and marketing teams—not a consumer mistake.
- Along the same lines, do you know how consumers research and learn about new brands and products? The Kearney Consumer Institute has found that many companies just *think* they know. Yet this knowledge of your customers will help determine the best way for you to listen and communicate with them.[2]
- Remember that customers may respond only when they are super-satisfied or super-unhappy with their purchase. You'll end up with the equivalent of a lot of 1- and 5-star ratings. But the really valuable reviews are the mediocre ones. These are customers who generally enjoy the product but see one or several major flaws that they often communicate in a constructive matter.
- Finally, remember that this is not a marketing instrument. There's no need to brag about yourself or manipulate how people respond. For example, don't provide incentives for positive feedback, such as discounts for positive reviews.

But when you follow these rules, you create resilience. After all, when customer preferences change, or when demand spikes, it creates a need for your company to pivot. The closer you follow customer sentiment, the faster you can recognize these changes, and the faster you can pivot. Furthermore, if you have design flaws or quality issues, you need to know about them so that you can address them.

Customer feedback also helps in product portfolio decisions. Which product ranges should you expand? Where should you invest? Which products should you drop? The more data you have, the more confidently you can answer these questions.

## Leverage Advanced Analytics in Customer Engagements Through Demand Sensing

Talking to individual customers is very old school. We're into *old school*—after all, we're making this book available in traditional paper-based formats! But new technologies also lead to new approaches, which you shouldn't ignore either. You can gain power and scope.

In the early 2000s, when people talked about your product, it was hard to listen in. Now it's much easier. You need to invest in analytics technologies such as these:

- **Data mining:** analyzing huge databases to develop insights and predictions
- **Web crawling:** identifying, scraping, and aggregating the most relevant data sources
- **Sentiment analysis:** understanding not only consumers' perspectives of your brand versus your competitors but also the sentiments driving those perceptions
- **Natural language processing:** using AI to recognize voice and text expressions

Rather than invest internally, you may hire a firm that knows how to use these technologies. Either way, with these forms of advanced analytics, you can turn customer feedback into meaningful insights.

Your first step is to identify what type of data you and your customers generate online. How do they find your products? How do they choose sizes, flavors, or other features? Can you get data on how they actually use the product?

Your second step is to identify the capabilities and talent you need. All this new data analysis requires more skilled people than you probably have on staff right now. If you want to get serious, you will have to reskill or hire.

Then you can build a database. What information can you link? What patterns emerge? You can start with basic statistical analysis. But eventually your company will need to hire or build expertise in data analytics.

Natural language processing and similar technologies can unlock the next level of demand sensing.

Now the question becomes what to do with the data. Probably the ideas will jump out at you. (See the sidebar, "An Airline Changes Its Reputation.") But if not, here are some ways to think about it: We often think of the crises that require resilience as affecting supply. Your supply chain is in crisis because of a pandemic or war or hurricane or alien invasion. But such crises can also affect demand. And any unexpected changes in demand stress your supply chain. By deploying advanced analytics, you can expect them. You can react in near–real time to changing customer preferences and demand shocks.

---

### AN AIRLINE CHANGES ITS REPUTATION

In 2020, a large airliner collected approximately 10 million tweets. Using *sentiment analysis*—looking at the language of the tweets—it coded them as positive, neutral, or negative. It plotted sentiment across the year. Then it compared its results to those of other airlines.

Not surprisingly, every time a new COVID-19 regulation came into effect, causing delays and cancellations, customer sentiment dropped. But the airline was surprised to discover that it fared worse than its competitors. Its customer sentiments dropped more severely during these crises than other airlines.

The airline dug more deeply into the data. It used *topic modelling* to cluster the tweets into 10 main themes based on the co-occurrence of words. Some of the themes included *delay, cancellation, rebooking, customer service,* and *catering*. This analysis showed that the themes driving customer frustration were rebooking and customer service.

All airlines experienced significant delays and cancellations during the pandemic. But this airline learned that it was not performing as well at supporting its passengers during the rebooking process. The passengers' travel experience was worse, which made them less likely to buy tickets in the future. In other words, other airlines fared better at *customer resilience* in the face of a crisis.

Armed with this knowledge, the airline reevaluated its rebooking and customer service processes.

*Demand sensing* is the process by which retailers make decisions about inventory, distribution, and sales, using information on market trends and what consumers want. In recent years, tried-and-true demand sensing methods have failed in the face of volatility. The results have been stock-outs, too much of the wrong inventory, and/or attempts to sell through the wrong channels.

The solution is partly technical: an approach that merges AI-backed sensing and predictive analytics with human feedback and customization. But it also requires a commitment to listen to consumers—to find the data that will unlock the insights. For example, when a global consumer health care company improved its demand sensing capabilities, it started tracking indicators for sales, supply, promotions, media coverage, pricing, customer reviews, content, keywords, and market share. Its forecasts improved within weeks of implementing the new demand sensing model. The project added an estimated equivalent of $24 million in incremental revenue based on the company's newfound ability to quickly pivot to respond to market changes.[3]

There are some pitfalls, as in all analytics efforts:

- Be wary of overinterpretation. You're looking for a story in data, but correlation may not imply causation. Once you see a story, review it critically. What are the risks and benefits of acting on it? Does this judgment fit your experience?
- Data itself has risks. To prevent data loss, be sure to follow best principles of cybersecurity. To prevent rights infringement, follow privacy law, remembering that it may be tighter in Europe than elsewhere.
- Keep in mind that these numbers are mere abstractions of your customers—data analytics should never replace direct contact.

Nevertheless, data can give you improved knowledge of customers. Whether you're thinking about tomorrow's innovations or responding to this morning's social media crisis, knowledge of customers helps you be resilient.

## Re-Engineer Your Product Portfolio Based on What Really Drives Customer Value

As many companies analyzed their pandemic supply chain failures, they found obvious culprits: shutdowns and mismatches and what some people might call signs of a coming apocalypse. But some also found a hidden culprit more within their control: complexity. In a crisis, complexity makes management harder. And complexity in operations is often driven by large portfolios of complex, feature-laden products.

If complexity was truly needed to drive sales, then it would be worth the risk. But does your company really know which of those products, and which of those features, actually create customer value?

You have two questions, which may or may not be linked:

- Which **features** of a product drive customer value? In the *design-to-value* process, you make sure that you include what the customer wants, and exclude what the customer doesn't want. It's not just about brand and price. With the right approaches and tools, you can learn the relative importance of various product features, and even customers' willingness to pay for various features. This is incredibly valuable information, but to reap the benefits, you need to both understand the customer and have internal processes that enable this understanding to shape design.
- Which **products** in your portfolio drive customer value? Which stock-keeping units (SKUs) really drive your growth? You may have heard of *product portfolio rationalization,* and its key insight that your *important* products are not necessarily your most popular ones. Some products may be cannibalizing others. The wealth of data you're now collecting about your customers can provide new insights. But we believe that best practices go beyond *rationalizing* your portfolio, to *modularizing* it.

The best way to understand *design to value* is to realize that any design effort has priorities. Kearney's Product Excellence and Renewal Lab (PERLab; https://www.kearney.com/product-design-data-platforms/

product-excellence-and-renewal-lab) is always asking clients: first, what are you designing *for*? The priority may be *cost* (in the past it *has* probably been cost), but it could be *value, sustainability, resilience,* or some other priority. In fact, it's always a combination of priorities—nobody has ever said, "Make it sustainable, and I don't care what it costs!" But the value of acknowledging these priorities is that you can pause before the design process to explicitly ask, What are my design goals? Perhaps those goals should be the aspects of the product that customers most value. Or maybe I'm designing for resilience, so I should favor materials that are more abundant or components that are less prone to breaking.

Knowing your priorities helps you make choices. For example, if battery life drives value, then maybe you don't need a brighter display. If taste drives value, then you can streamline the packaging. You don't have to *deemphasize* the packaging, just *streamline* it. The packaging can still communicate the product's wonderful taste. But a major goal for the packaging becomes reducing its contribution to operations complexity.

Kearney clients also do plenty of *portfolio rationalization*. In these projects, we ask, What types of product groups do you have, and how are they developing? Then within each product group, how are different SKUs developing? Do you really need so many different variations? This is a place to leverage your rich customer data. You can simulate what would happen if you reduced, say, 20 SKUs to 15, or 10. In which cases would customers be willing to substitute a different SKU, and in which cases would you lose the sale? Meanwhile, how would reducing SKUs change your contribution margins and fixed costs?

This is where these projects often run aground. Rationalizing a portfolio is relatively quick and easy, but it always has revenue implications. You can mitigate those implications to get the most out of your trade-off, but it is still a trade-off. The sales department won't be happy. Thus, when appropriate, Kearney's PERLab prefers to talk about a *modular* portfolio. When you go modular, the goal is to have the same diversity of products, but with less complexity.

To take an oversimplified example, imagine that you make water bottles. Some customers like to drink from a built-in straw; others don't. You could rationalize your portfolio by telling salespeople that the non-straw drinkers can just ignore the straw. But in a modular design, you simply put different lids on the same bottle. The key is to get the *interface* right—to make sure that both lids screw onto the bottle the same way.

This modularization is the way to move toward the platform principles discussed in Chapter 3—creating products out of fungible building blocks. For example, the Turkish appliance-maker Arçelik has introduced a modular product architecture to increase commonality across its products. It has simplified spare parts management and reduced lead times, tooling costs, and procurement complexity.[4]

Certainly all decisions about products and their features are thorny. Customers are fickle. Before you make drastic changes, you need to test the data thrice. You need to confirm your analyses with additional data sources such as consumer studies. And as the Kearney Consumer Institute (KCI; https://www.kearney.com/consumer-retail/kearney-consumer-institute) found, you need to keep in mind that your customers may not define quality or convenience the way you think they do. For example, consumers often pinpoint a *primary* quality for a category of items. When buying jeans, they equate quality with *fit* and *comfort*. A jeans maker may see quality in terms of *style, durability,* or *sustainability,* but emphasizing these various components of quality creates complexity. You need to know your customers well enough to realize that some of this complexity doesn't create value.[5]

KCI also found that consumers define convenience *as part of full brand experience.* They want it to be fast (enough) and easy (enough) given the context. A 20-minute wait means something very different at a fast-food joint versus a trendy new restaurant. For some types of groceries, *convenience* may mean home delivery, but for others, it's more convenient to pop into the store and grab what you need.[6]

Thus your efforts to understand customer-product relationships are always cross-functional. The value of a product comes not only from its design features but also from the sales experience and the quality of the inputs. So design needs support from sales, R&D, and procurement. Likewise, portfolio rationalization needs support from sales.

There's always tension here: marketing wants 500 variations of a product, and operations wants just one. Managing that tension to find a solution (presumably somewhere in the middle) is how you demonstrate your leadership skills.

At its best, this journey to accomplish the twin efforts of designing for value and simplifying portfolio complexity brings you so close to customers that you transform your whole company. For example, Unox, an Italy-based global manufacturer of commercial ovens, sold through dealers, was so challenged to learn more about its user base. When it started putting Internet of Things sensors in its ovens, it learned that customers didn't use the ovens the way Unox expected. So it developed a mobile app showing ways to use the oven effectively, and as a result, it found that customers used their ovens 30% more. Then it developed a "monitor fleet" app to help chain stores that had to bake the same thing the same way every day everywhere. Also a recipe management app to help restaurant chains synchronize recipe updates across multiple sites. And a kitchen scheduling app to help large kitchens (such as those at hospitals) improve efficiency. What did customers value about Unox ovens? In at least some cases, it was apps! Furthermore, the apps collected additional information (with user permission, of course). Unox used all this information to make design changes for new ovens—including new revenue streams for premium support. It has improved retention and upselling; it has reduced support costs because now it can provide more support remotely instead of onsite. In some ways, Unox has transformed itself from an oven manufacturer to a baking partner. That makes its customer relationships far different, richer, and more resilient.[7]

But even if you don't go that far, design to value improves resilience because a streamlined product is less costly and less complex. Fewer features likely means fewer parts, fewer suppliers, fewer processes, fewer assembly sites—in short, fewer risks across the supply chain. Likewise with product portfolio efforts: you don't have extra parts to add to the product or extra processes for all the different sizes or flavors. Furthermore, you free up inventory space, resources, and working capital. All are valuable when you need to flex in a crisis.

# Build an Omnichannel Strategy to Ensure Order Fulfilment

In the heart of Wyoming's beef country, Greybull Valley Produce grows lettuce in hydroponic gardens. Founded in 2017, this family-owned small business found success selling to area restaurants and schools. Then came the pandemic. "We lost 90 percent of our business overnight," owner Dwight Koehn told the *Greybull Standard* in 2021. It needed other channels in which to sell its greens. So it approached grocery stores in Montana, and adjusted its fulfillment processes to incorporate the 300-mile round trip. The plan worked. Then, when restaurants and schools reopened post-pandemic, Greybull Valley Produce had greatly expanded its customer base and was poised for growth.[8]

There were thousands of these stories in the pandemic. A European vineyard that sold to restaurants created an online shop to sell to end consumers. A Peruvian fish distributor launched a local door-to-door local delivery service. A global outdoor brand that sold mostly through dedicated retail stores shifted inventory from the closed stores to its online fulfillment channels. In a crisis, these companies quickly shifted channels.

Before the next crisis hits, it's worth thinking about channels and growth—and reducing operations complexity.

Since the invention of e-commerce a few decades ago, retailers have been struggling with the *omnichannel challenge*. Sometimes consumers like to buy online, sometimes in a store. Yet they want the transition to be totally seamless: order online and pick it up in the store—or if it doesn't work, return it to the store. Buy it in the store and then return it by mail, or return it to a different store. Order it by phone and then track it online, or track it in person while visiting the store.

It's a headache to manage all this information to be available anywhere, anytime. It's also a headache to manage all the logistics, warehouse, and cloud operations behind all that. And the pandemic demonstrated that these sorts of headaches are coming for all sorts of non-retail companies as well.

Once customers see *multiple* channels, they want more. They want seamlessness. Thus *multichannel* business—selling your vineyard's wine to both restaurants and online end consumers—may not be enough. In many industries, you need to work on integration to achieve *omnichannel*. Your strategy will vary considerably depending on your situation: what you make, how you sell it, what your customers want, and what your competitors are doing. But for many companies, omnichannel operations will be at the heart of their efforts to be more resilient for the customer. (See the sidebar, "The Great Pandemic Toilet Paper Shortage and the Challenges of Omnichannel Retailing.")

---

**THE GREAT PANDEMIC TOILET PAPER SHORTAGE AND THE CHALLENGES OF OMNICHANNEL RETAILING**

The much-publicized mid-pandemic toilet paper shortages resulted partly from hoarding, but also from the pitfalls of changing channels. There was plenty of toilet paper available. The problem was that most of it was in the big rolls destined for office buildings, college campuses, restaurants, and airports. It was scratchy, utilitarian stuff shipped in huge pallets rather than consumer-friendly packs. It was a different product, often with a different supply chain. "Shifting to retail channels," journalist Will Oremus wrote, required "new relationships and contracts between suppliers, distributors, and stores; different formats for packaging and shipping; new trucking routes—all for a bulky product with lean profit margins."[9]

Since the early 2000s, many retailers expanded from brick-and-mortar to online, or vice versa. They can talk at great length about the pitfalls of the multichannel supply chain: lost sales and high costs due to siloed inventory, duplication of effort, lack of flexibility, and customer frustration. Yet when you seek to overcome the *multichannel* pitfalls by going *omnichannel*, by mixing everything together, you face new pitfalls. For example, when you send items from a warehouse to replenish a store, you want pallets, cases, and/or totes, because all the peanut butter goes on the same shelf. But when you're filling an online order from that warehouse, the parcels will be mixed, peanut butter and jelly. This requires an *eaches* order fulfillment process, the opposite of the case-oriented process. Mixing the processes is inefficient.

Furthermore, although retailers can most efficiently replenish a national peanut butter brand through large regional distribution centers, an artisan delivers her small-batch marmalade directly to the local store. How then does the store fulfill online orders for marmalade? Does it ship marmalade to be cross-docked at the warehouse? Does it split the order, shipping half from the warehouse and half from the store? Or does it try to foist these complicated decisions off on to the customer or artisan?[10]

Some retail chains have made great progress on these questions. For example, the Home Depot invested in cars, vans, and flatbed trucks, supported by 150 new fulfillment centers and cross-dock locations. Kroger built nine large, automated regional fulfillment centers linked to new cross-docks and delivery vans, with some delivery outsourced to Instacart and Shipt. The key is to focus on your commercial objectives rather than assets and technology. You need an interconnected, fit-for-purpose response to evolving demand patterns, which makes the customer the top priority without losing sight of business objectives and the end goal of profitable growth.[11]

In short, this is one of our favorite examples of the tension between operating for the customer and simplifying operations. You *can* find a balanced omnichannel solution—indeed, in some industries, you *must*—but it will require work.

Everyone starts from a different baseline. How is your current supply chain set up? Where are your customers? Where are your warehouses and distribution centers? What can your IT infrastructure handle? (This is a huge challenge—maybe even a book on its own.) Are there regional differences? How do customers currently buy your products, and how do you fulfill those orders? These answers will differ greatly depending on your industry. But this knowledge—especially of the customer journey—can help you understand which channels to push.

Next, consider options. What other distribution channels are available? How do they fit with your company's strategic orientation? (This likely requires discussions with the C-suite.) Then you can prepare a business case for the channels you want to develop.

Intertwined with the omnichannel challenge is the challenge of last-mile delivery. They're both big, thorny problems. But thinking about them *together* can increase resilience. For example, the data flows you need to solve last-mile delivery are also providing you with more opportunities for control in the upstream supply chain. Or if you encourage customers to pick items up at the store, they may be tempted to buy something while they're there. These richer relationships—with your customers and your data—give you more room to pivot in a crisis.

And again, that sort of resilience is your goal. By developing the ability to seamlessly switch among distribution channels, you will be able to fulfill orders even when specific channels are disrupted. You can retain your customer base even when their shopping habits significantly change.

## Move Closer to the End-Consumer to Sell "in the Region, for the Region"

In a sense, across this entire book we're arguing that resilience requires *intimacy*. You want more intimacy with your suppliers so that you can better understand their problems before those problems become yours. You want more intimacy with your customers so that you can better understand their needs and fulfill them. Both of these stances represent paradigm shifts from common understandings of the lean approach, in which intimacy might hinder the desired transactional nature of your relationships.

One way to improve intimacy is through geography. Chapter 8 explored ways to bring your suppliers geographically closer to operations (and customers). It's good because it reduces logistics risks—but it's also good because it increases intimacy. Here we'll continue the argument. Bringing your operations (and suppliers) closer to customers reduces risks and, more importantly, increases intimacy.

By moving closer to end customers, you will be able to better serve their needs. Most obviously, you can reduce lead times. This was the first lesson of fast fashion as discussed in Chapter 3: by producing domestically, fast-fashion disrupters could more quickly get the latest styles into their customers' closets. As consumer impatience grows across many sectors—and as your competitors invest in ways to satisfy it—the lesson expands far beyond the fashion industry.

Chapter 8's discussion of moving your suppliers closer to your factory implicitly assumed that the factory was close (enough) to customers. Now we're saying it's worth looking at the factory location as well. If your company is global, you may have multiple regional factories. They will support multiple regional customer markets. And they'll be supported by multiple regional supply chains (often called *multi-local* supply chains).

That may require more management effort on your part. But it's taking advantage of wider cultural trends. You have more tools available to ease that management burden. You have more data available to customize products and processes by region. And in many cases your customers have more money available to spend on exactly what they want, rather than a mass-produced global item that only comes vaguely close to what they want. (See the sidebar, "Reshoring *to* China!?!")

---

### RESHORING *TO* CHINA!?!

In this chapter, specifically, we're talking about the business benefits of gaining intimacy with your customers by locating your operations closer to them. If your customers are in the US, you might reshore operations to the US (or nearshore near the US). If your customers are in China, you might reshore operations from other countries **to China**.

A leading global apparel company did exactly this. Following the logic of the lowest-cost supply chain, it had, decades ago, developed operations in China. Then, as incomes increased, it moved its operations to Southeast Asian countries with lower labor costs.

Yet as Chinese incomes increase, Chinese consumers buy more apparel. China now accounts for almost one-quarter of this company's global sales. To increase its share of the Chinese apparel market, it studied Chinese consumers. It found a market defined by "fashion and speed." Chinese consumers want fashionable products and fast updates. (They're classic fast-fashion consumers as described in Chapter 3.) So the company piloted a series of quick-response (QR) products. Some of these QR products were locally designed, with simple fabrics. They were fashionable, which was why speed was so critical. But they weren't performance products, needing many technical

*(continued)*

(*continued*)

adjustments, and thus the time frames and expertise of existing manu-facturing sites.

Other QR products were not necessarily locally designed but were produced locally for in-season quick replenishment. The definition of a QR product was that it was locally produced. Transferring production from Southeast Asia to China could increase costs by 8 to 20%. But the benefit of reducing lead times made up for it. The company also reduced transport costs for both materials and finished goods, because the overseas factories had been importing most of their synthetic fabrics from China.

The pilot project succeeded wildly. The company now produces locally 75% of its apparel sold in China. Though its localization efforts paused in 2020–2022 due to pandemic uncertainties, it is planning more increases in local production going forward. It is not alone. Its global competitors are all maintaining or increasing their domestic Chinese production levels—none are decreasing.

The company's strategy ripples out across its operations. For example, it now pre-stocks in China certain materials that are likely to be used in local designs. It's more likely to choose partners based on capabilities rather than lowest costs. It adjusted its business model to center on rapid response to the market. And it's exploring QR pilot projects in other regions.

To get started, pull out the maps. Where is your customer base concentrated? How far are those customers from your manufacturing and supply base? How many geographic customer concentrations do you have?

Next, consider what might happen next. What are the demand forecasts? How's the geopolitical situation? Any expected changes in the regulatory framework? Answers to these questions may help determine if it makes sense to pull out of specific markets, or into others. Where do you need to double down? And how does this relate to your omnichannel strategy?

Now you can select the markets where "in the region, for the region" makes sense. Start to draft a multiyear road map to make it happen.

This road map should be realistic; any reshoring effort will drive costs and complexity. By reversing the decades-long trend toward offshoring, you're going to pay more for labor and for supplies. In many cases, these higher costs can be balanced by higher product availability, shorter lead times, reduced transportation requirements, an improved focus on customer value, and/or lower risks—but you do still have to keep costs under control. In particular, a multi-local supply chain will also create organizational complexity. You'll need more people to do additional management—and overhead costs have an unfortunate habit of spiraling.

Multi-local supply chains do better when you simultaneously multi-localize suppliers. In other words, if you build five factories close to customers, but they all still depend on faraway suppliers, you won't gain many resilience benefits. You'll just push risk factors upstream while needlessly complicating your operations.

However, if you do successfully implement the multi-local supply chain, you risk creating silos. You risk de-standardization. When it comes time to update the product—perhaps for safety or sustainability concerns—your multi-local updates will suffer from a time-consuming lack of scale.

Yet these risks are worth taking because you can build resilience. When you're closer to customers, you're less susceptible to bad weather, natural disasters, clogged ports, or other logistics risks. You are also more resilient against changes in policy. For example, if you produce locally, you don't have to worry about local content requirements. Finally, producing locally means that you are *culturally* closer to your customers. You can connect better with them because you share experiences and outlooks. The events that uniquely alter your customers' attitudes—a drought, a celebrity trend, or God forbid a terrorist act—have also altered your employees' attitudes. Because you know what's happening, and why, you can react more quickly.

CHAPTER 10

# Create Resilient Teams by Combining Expertise into Economies of Skill

Building a resilient workforce is essential. But dealing with people and culture issues can be hard because they're so unique to your particular situation. Rather than data-driven initiatives, you may need to rely on broader sets of skills. Here are five approaches to consider.

## Make Time to Listen to Your People—What Bothers Them Should Bother You

In the 19th century, your biggest assets were physical: a factory, a mine, a farm, an oceangoing vessel. In the 21st century, no matter what business you're in, you're in the people business. Even as physical assets become more sophisticated—automated assembly lines needing less grunt labor— they are more dependent on the knowledgeable employees in control.

For example, that oceangoing vessel has evolved into a sophisticated supply chain. Yet to build resilient supply chains, you need to build resilient teams. And you need to pay as much attention to your teams as to your physical assets. To get data on predictive maintenance of your physical assets, you can invest in sensors and networks (as we will discuss in Chapter 11). To get data on your people, you already have the sensors you need—ears.

Make time to listen to your team. Presumably you already *talk* to them, about work. But you also need to *listen:* create opportunities for them to share problems or worries. To give them a feeling of safety, try to do this outside of regular work meetings or feedback sessions. Optimally, you can set up 30–60 minutes with your direct reports every week or two. This will give them an opportunity to vent and also enables you to get to know them better. This is time you're investing in knowledge of your people and operations.

It's not necessarily easy, especially given post-pandemic changing conditions of work, when the team isn't necessarily in the same location as you. But that's what makes it important. And note that the pandemic had disproportionate negative effects on women. In addition to higher job departures (both voluntary and involuntary), in a hybrid working model women have reported being excluded from formal and informal discussions, experiencing reduced visibility to senior leaders, and, as a result, facing more limited professional opportunity. So these types of conversations are essential to both employee retention and your diversity, equity, and inclusion (DEI) priorities.[1]

After all, it's not just the pandemic. Every disruption tests the resilience of your people. Constant firefighting mode can be exhausting. People quit because they're burned out. By listening to their concerns, you can identify the symptoms earlier. How can they do less firefighting? How can they feel more productive? How can you not burn them out? By cultivating a culture where people share problems with you, you will gain greater transparency into all sorts of potential issues (including the stuff they once tried to hide from you). Transparency builds resilience. The empowerment you give them builds resilience.

If this sort of activity doesn't come naturally to you, keep in mind some ground rules:

- Offer it, but don't force it. Maybe it's not the culture at your firm. You do need to change that culture, but it won't happen overnight.

- Don't use these meetings to give feedback or assign work tasks. "The report is due tomorrow and your last one was insufficient but, oh yeah, tell me how you're doing" is not going to get you what you need.
- You may think it would be more efficient to do this in a group meeting but again that's not how it works.
- If your employees don't want to have these sessions, accept it. Maybe they just don't want to talk. The most important thing is that they know that this is an option.

You can start by mapping your direct contacts. What's a schedule that would work for you and them? Reach out individually to discuss the option. Make sure to frame it as appreciation and support rather than control or micromanagement. It's fine to change the cadence, length, or tone after the first few sessions. The point is to find a mode that works for you and your team.

Some companies choose to highlight listening not only among direct reports but also communities of interest. For example, Stitch Fix, an online personal style service, developed employee resource groups that are billed as "safe, internal spaces for groups that have experienced systemic exclusion from opportunity." Each community has two coleads who are supported by the firm to carry out the role, receive a special equity grant each year as compensation for their contributions, and are recognized internally for their leadership.[2]

But it doesn't have to be formal. Charlene Thomas, a 33-year leader at UPS, notes that in almost every job she's had, her first step was to connect with her new team ("Meet them in their environment. Get to know the people—their strengths, weaknesses, and relationships with each other."). Her goal: "Listen for understanding." Listening was the base from which she could empower teams to solve problems and remove barriers they faced.[3]

## Hire Diverse—Not Only from Different Fields but Also from Different Backgrounds

Here's some wisdom about diversity. "The true strength of this firm, as in any organization, lies in the fact that we are all different....The strength inherent in this firm rests upon these collective and diverse interests. They are all we have."[4]

The quote comes from our company's founder, Tom Kearney. He said it more than 80 years ago—which highlights the enduring wisdom of diversity *as resilience*. Tom Kearney believed that diversity led to resilient strength, even though his definition of diversity was much different than ours today. Today the world defines diversity more broadly and rigorously, but diversity still leads to resilient strength.

Diversity can relate to the background of a person: gender, ethnicity, culture, upbringing. It can also refer to their professional background, or their skills. You want to hire people with diverse backgrounds—for example, businesspeople for tech jobs, and vice versa. More specifically, in operations, you want to hire for skills from planning to delivery, and from leadership to technology. When you encounter a problem, your ideal solution will come from a team that thinks about it in different ways: introverts plus extroverts, systems thinkers plus intuitives, theoreticians plus those grounded in the weeds. A background in an unrelated field, or an unusual or lacking skill set, is a major plus.

Operations in particular benefits from diverse skill sets. It's extremely helpful to have engineers with business experience, operations managers who understand technology, and data scientists who are anchored in your specific products and business models. As you seek to improve operations resilience, you want your people to see a bigger picture. And when they see that picture from different perspectives—including the perspectives of previously marginalized communities—your team is much more easily able to recognize and build consensus on new challenges and creative solutions.

To start, review the backgrounds of your current teams. Do you have different perspectives? Or is it all homogeneous? Map out which perspectives and backgrounds are completely lacking in your team. Now look at your open position(s). Who are the candidates being considered? How can they add to your diversity? Can you talk to HR to tailor future job ads toward these skills?

Of course you won't pursue tokenism just to increase diversity key performance indicators (KPIs). It's not about getting one person for each field or each country or each sexual orientation or each generation.

You're still focusing on capabilities and qualifications—diversity is not sufficient reason to make an unqualified hire.

And diversity is not only about hiring. The more diverse your team, the easier it is to run into misunderstandings or cultural conflicts. So if you are able to get a diverse team in place, hooray!—but your job is not over. How are you going to manage the culture? How will you ensure that members of traditionally marginalized communities feel valued? How will you help members of traditionally privileged communities change their behavior, without feeling picked on or pushed out? How will you get both the new hires and the holdovers to stay, and contribute? You accomplish that management by maintaining an open and supportive atmosphere. In other words, you listen to your people, and act on that knowledge, as described in the previous section ("Make Time to Listen to Your People—What Bothers Them Should Bother You").

The reason you do all this work is that your team is stronger for having different skills and perspectives available. You will likely be able to identify problems faster and discuss them from different angles. You will also be able to combine skills to find out-of-the-box solutions on the fly. You will solve complex problems more quickly.

## Build an Extended Learning Curriculum for Targeted Development of Your Team

Some people talk about a *fourth industrial revolution*, some about the sustainability imperative. Some people talk about demographics: half the world's population is younger than 30 years old. And some people talk about the results of globalization, in which worldwide flows affect not only markets for goods and data but also markets for labor.[5]

Yet, however you talk about it, the message is clear: future ways of working will be different. For example, depending on your industry and situation, you may discover that ideas of *jobs* give way to *tasks*, and *employees* to *value contributions*. Traditional hierarchies may give way to venture capital–inspired organizational structures such as a "team of teams." And of course hybrid approaches to work-from-home flexibility are here to stay.[6] So how will you help your employees adjust?

For example, an automotive OEM with presence in Eastern Europe was struggling with the availability of skilled labor. A lack of digital talent was becoming a bottleneck for its efforts to drive smart manufacturing. So it expanded its training curriculum and increased the number of training days per employee. The new curriculum focused on soft and hard skills and had a strong focus on digital applications and data analytics. It was open to shop floor as well as office workers and presented multiple career paths so they had choices about their specialization. The company invested significant time and money—but within a few years, it had significantly upskilled its regional workforce. It was able to recruit talent mostly internally. It also saw a significant uptick in employee retention and satisfaction, and in applications.

Every firm has a training curriculum. But is your curriculum up-to-date? Too often, it doesn't even reflect *current* conditions, much less future ways of working. So start by reviewing it. Is it balanced? Is it meaningful? Ask your employees what works well and what they are lacking. Amid the current war for talent, are your training budgets adequate?

You may discover that you need to collaborate with HR in a redesign. You want a curriculum that will boost the strengths and counteract the weaknesses of your teams. Focus on hard skills—especially digital skills!—as well as soft skills. And be sure to take advantage of technology. Under old ways of working and learning, lectures and course readings proliferated because they were the most scalable approaches to disseminating information. But now you have more options. For example, the Bank of Ireland's Careers Lab is a digital platform for learning, development, and mentorship. It uses gamification such as badges and challenges, it encourages development of virtual communities, and it has special talent programs for women and ethnic minorities.[7]

You'll likely want to focus on lifelong learning. Talented people want to continue to grow and challenge their talents. Companies that become learning organizations are well set up to attract and retain them. But this means that you need to think about a development path that serves the interests of both the company and the employee. Such training isn't role specific, such as technical briefings for engineers. Nor is it a random assortment of unrelated topics. Instead you are helping employees to broaden their horizon and get new perspectives on their own challenges.

You may well shift to more "snackable content" in the form of retreats and immersion, e-learning platforms, academies, simulation centers, and learning hubs/campuses.[8]

When training is done poorly, it's abysmal. Everyone knows the content is out-of-date or irrelevant. Remote attendees turn off their cameras so that they can read emails. Internal trainers may lack expertise or charisma. The whole thing can feel feels like a giant waste of time that people have to endure to satisfy HR.

But when training is done well, employees gain a better sense of development and career progression, which improves their satisfaction. They gain skills that they can use to meet challenges head on, which will lead to more resilient operations. Meanwhile, the company develops an internal source for top talent. This homegrown approach ensures that you always have a baseline of highly qualified candidates when you're trying to fill a position.

## Map Your Talent Globally and Set up Global Expert Exchanges

The word *silo* comes from the Greek *siros*, meaning "a pit to keep grain in." In 1873, American farmer Fred Hatch built the first *tower silo*, which had advantages in using gravity for compaction. But believe it or not, today more such silos are built in business than farming. Tower silos present all sorts of operational dangers, and many farmers now use *bag silos*, which are basically 10-foot-long plastic tubes that lay on the ground. But businesses keep building ever taller and more impenetrable metaphorical towers in which to hide away valuable expertise.[9]

Indeed, for many global firms, a key challenge is simply understanding the depth and breadth of expertise they already have in the company. There may be good reasons to use different solutions to operational challenges at different locations—but there's often a lot to learn from sharing, too. Too often, an employee who is presented with a challenge doesn't even know where to look for help.

Thus a first step is to define what type of expertise is relevant in your organization. You may want to build a category tree covering, for example, technical, industry, business, and analytics skills. Next, you establish a baseline of your global expertise. One way to construct this map is to conduct a survey, asking teams to self-report. Another approach is to work outside-in, based on job profiles and CVs. Either way, you want to understand what knowledge resides where in the company.

Then you want to figure out how to *use* that knowledge. Approaches may include one or more of the following:

- **An expert database.** Knowledge wants to be shared, and sharing best practices and use cases between functions and units can help you disseminate best standards. A database is an easy way to collect that knowledge. However, setting up the database is an arduous task that requires up-front buy-in and support from a variety of experts. If only half the experts provide insights, users won't get into the habit of consulting the database. And then you have to keep it up-to-date!
- **Intranet features.** Depending on your situation, you may have avenues to deploy expertise on your intranet. Remember, you can't hide expertise—the knowledge has to be available even to lower-level managers. So find meaningful ways for them to access experts. If there's too much red tape, they won't use it, but if you're too lenient, your experts will get swamped.
- **A root mentality.** In the previous section ("Build an Extended Learning Curriculum for Targeted Development of Your Team"), we mentioned how some companies are moving from a *hierarchy* to a *tree*. In such cultures, rather than supervising, executives are *enabling*, often by connecting employees to resources and knowledge. They serve as that database in human form.
- **A dedicated talent management function.** Again, these are people whose job it is to empower employees by making connections and filling in knowledge.
- **A global expert exchange.** Think of the *faculty lunch* at a small college—all of the professors benefit from hearing how one of their colleagues does a deep dive into her expertise. In other words, you do need a formalized setting, such as one expert presenting a topic once per month. You do want to have the events moderated. And you

should allow lots of junior employees to join, because they can learn something from listening in.

For example, a global manufacturer of construction machines had some manufacturing plants in Central/Eastern Europe and some in Southeast Asia. It realized that the two business units had begun to operate as silos. Both units ran well, but they never shared best practices. Worse, they were starting to get de-standardized. Each unit would revise product specifications to fit changing needs. So the company asked each unit to map their expertise in different roles. Then, global leadership started to host monthly sharing sessions for experts from both sides to come together and discuss thought leadership on a given topic. In the monthly procurement sharing session, commodity managers for specific categories shared their supplier strategy, their main vendors, their five-year strategy, and the tools they used. Managers of other commodities listened in. Simply learning about lessons—in negotiations, spec simplifications, and other issues—prompted commodity managers to contemplate and implement best practices. Furthermore, subject matter experts gained better internal visibility between the two units, which helped with allocating the right expertise to future projects.

In short, *knowing where to find an expert* is an incredibly valuable source of resilience in a critical situation. Too many firms spend too long identifying expertise, or buy it externally, or decide to forgo it completely. But when your experts are linked, and best practices shared, your solutions gain power. You have to suffer a specific supply chain vulnerability only once in a unit, rather than once in *every* unit.

## Let People Find Their Purpose—and Let the Sum of Individual Purpose Define Your Culture

As humans, we spend nearly 50% of our waking hours working (or getting ready for work or commuting to and from work). Work should be more than just a series of tasks we perform every day in order to not starve. Work should enable each of us to fulfill a sense of purpose. For example, some people have a unique ability to spot patterns. They gain a sense of fulfillment in seeing patterns that indicate a change in demand or supply. When these people have operations jobs, they're finding a sense of purpose in their work.

Most companies try to cultivate some sort of purpose in their employees. They usually do so through top-down communication of a vision or a set of cultural values. And plenty of us have been drawn to an organization, or have stayed long term, because of these visions or values. But there are an awful lot of people for whom this stuff feels deeply irrelevant. "Those are the firm's values," they say, "not mine."

What do you do with such employees? You could try to "convert" them by proclaiming your vision and culture at louder volumes, but the issue isn't that they didn't hear you. It's that they didn't connect. So you could let them plod along, disconnected. But surely this was the impetus behind the "trends" of the great resignation and quiet quitting—the pandemic reminded people that they should feel fulfilled by work, and if they didn't, they should walk away.

So what if you let your people find their own purpose? Let them define what the job and the organization mean to them. Why they show up for work every day. Instead of telling them about vision and values, you listen to understand. Then you let the sum of these individual purposes define your culture.

If this sounds too non-hierarchical, too haphazard, too disempowering for senior executives—remember, that's what the world is like today. You need resilience because the world is too non-hierarchical, haphazard, and disempowering of your most cherished plans. You build that resilience by building and empowering teams. And if you believe, as we do, that at least some of these challenges will require organizational transformation, then it's your everyday people who will enable the transformation to happen, who will nurture it inside out and bottom up.

To achieve this grassroots-purpose-driven culture, start by listening rather than talking. Don't presume that you know what your employees think. Maybe you use global townhall formats or other collective approaches to people sharing their views; maybe you deploy "culture days" or similar formats in workshops; maybe you use anonymous surveys to collect ideas and perspectives. Whatever the approach, you should allow for time for assimilation. New hires (whether they're junior analysts or CXOs) will need some time to understand your culture and purpose and relate it to their own. For that matter, longtime veterans may need time, too, because they've never been asked a question like this before. So everyone gets time and support in this process.

As soon as you know your employee's perspectives, put them vis-à-vis your currently formalized cultural values and vision. What is different? What is the same? Where can you be led by your team? Again, it takes time. You don't want to be volatile or jittery. It's good to crowdsource your culture, but not to redefine or rephrase it every year or two. The objective is to make your people feel included, not alienated; to lead by empowering, not abdicating.

Success on this journey will cultivate a sense of belonging in your employees. That means that they will not be as easily poached by competitors in the war for talent. Success will also make your teams more efficient. As your people find their own purpose reflected in the collective purpose, they are more likely to share issues and challenges with their team. Such strength itself improves resilience. It also enables resilient initiatives across the organization.

CHAPTER 11

# Combine Human and Artificial Intelligence to Build Resilience Through Constant Learning

To be resilient in a crisis, you need to make good judgments. Those judgments are informed by learning from experience. Technological tools such as artificial intelligence (AI) can combine with human intelligence (HI) to learn more effectively, more richly informed by data. Here are five ways to implement those ideas.

## Ensure an Efficient Data Flow and Build an AI/ Analytics Flywheel

Did you hear about the sign advertising National Procrastination Week? It didn't go up until Friday. But not because the sign painter procrastinated—there was a delay in getting her the specs and other data she needed. This has been the story of the last few decades: people get better and better at collecting more and more data ... and then discover the challenges in getting the right data to the right person at the right time. With the advent of AI, this conundrum will only grow. Data is useful only with efficient *flow*.

To help build efficient flow, we like to think about the *flywheel*. In mechanics, a flywheel is a very heavy wheel that generates and transfers energy to other parts of a machine. In *Good to Great*, Jim Collins wrote that corporate transformations can feel like starting a flywheel. It takes endless, persistent effort to complete just one turn. But eventually, as the flywheel builds speed, it develops nearly unstoppable momentum. Jeff Bezos loved the flywheel concept and used it to power the growth of Amazon.com.[1]

The flywheel is an especially valuable metaphor for today's technological revolutions for two reasons. First, you will exert a lot of effort and money to get going. Second, once it gets going, the flywheel—if designed correctly—will transfer energy across all your operations.

Jeff Bezos' genius wasn't that he read a book about flywheels and followed its advice. It was that he designed the ideal flywheel for his company's situation. Likewise, your decisions about how to set up your flywheel today will be the most important decisions you make.

One way to start is with the data: *which answers could I derive from this?* The other way is to start with your most pressing questions: *how could data answer them?* If you have a business (rather than tech or math) orientation, you may prefer the second approach. For example, in procurement, you may want answers to questions such as, Am I choosing from and dealing with the right set of suppliers? Are my chosen suppliers delivering what I think I am buying? Are my own internal stakeholder needs being met?[2]

Either way, you will soon be deep in data: What do we have? How is it cleaned, stored, tracked? Who has access to it? How is it (or should it be) connected to other data, internally and externally? These links among different data sources—the data flow—will take a lot of early thinking, especially if you have legacy systems. (See the sidebar, "The Single Source of Truth and Other Koans.")

## THE SINGLE SOURCE OF TRUTH AND OTHER KOANS

The *single source of truth* will be your bogeyman as you develop data analytics capabilities. Because it's a Zen koan: a riddle that is both profound and nonsensical, both impossible to solve and the key to solving everything. Data should provide you with a single source of truth across your enterprise and all your suppliers. Thus your efforts may fail because you didn't cleanse, authenticate, integrate, and perfect your data.

At the same time, nobody's data is or will ever be perfect. People from across the firm will take data—even data from a single source—and interpret it to fit preconceived narratives. So your efforts may fail because you assumed your data is uniquely perfect or because you wasted time trying to make it so.

Your data is amazing and powerful. But your data might be wrong. It might have errors, or you might err in interpreting it. For example, correlation often does not imply causation, so you need to apply common sense. How do the analytics compare with your expectations? Even if they confirm your suspicions, be careful. Getting started is when you are most vulnerable to confirmation bias.

Your data is all-encompassing. But your data will have gaps. So you need to acknowledge them and know how to work around them. Data gives answers that will be statistical rather than definitive: a percentage likelihood that a machine will break down, rather than a command to replace the machine next week. So you may need to add the meaningful analysis: what would a breakdown mean for production schedules, and what mitigation options would be available? Thus your success will depend not only on your data but also on the narratives and analyses you apply: whether they're true, whether they're appropriate to the situation, and whether the people who believe in them are capable of change in the face of contrary evidence.

The promise of data is that you will never again have to decide an issue by going with your gut. Yet no matter how good your data is, it can never make decisions for you. It is insights, rather than data alone, that builds resilience. To get the right insights, you must hone your judgments and decision-making skills. In short, the best use of data is to cultivate and refine your company's collective gut.

And in the ultimate koan, data and the AI tools you use to enhance it represent a set of technical tools that unlock trillion-dollar opportunities.

*(continued)*

> (*continued*)
>
> Yet any meaningful opportunity has to be a ***business*** rather than a ***technical*** project. To realize value—and to understand risks—your company needs structures and processes for people on the business side (all the way up to the board!) to understand and act based on those risks and benefits.[3]

To improve data flow, set up databases that link data points. Reach out to other teams to link databases. If you have to work in the environment that you already have—in other words, your existing enterprise resource planning (ERP) system—be mindful of its limitations. But now may be the time for you and your CIO to ask bigger questions. Maybe you should move to an *event-driven architecture*, an innovative approach to data integration.[4] Maybe you should explore a *data mesh* to accelerate data sharing across your organization. Data mesh amounts to a new strategy, operating model, and technical architecture—but its decentralized approach can deliver data-as-a-product to internal and external stakeholders, such as suppliers and customers.[5] And regardless of your data management structures and guidelines, the bigger issue is to foster a culture of data sharing and encourage all employees to improve their data thinking and understanding.

The gap between having data and using it is a bigger problem than many people realize. Many major organizations have set up a data lake—but use less than 5% of it. Because Internet of Things (IoT) sensors, online shopping, and industrial robots throw off so much data automatically, you probably have a ton of it. (The average volume of data collected increased by a factor of 14 from 2015 to 2020.) The cost of storing that data is continually falling. So the issue now becomes how to increase the *value* of that data through effective authentication and governance. For example, leading companies invest four times more in data reliability than laggards—and get six times better outcomes as a result.[6]

Once you have the data, you need to find ways to structure it, analyze it, and visualize it. Only then can you really use it. Of course, you also have to communicate it—get it to the right teams at the right times. By ensuring a better data exchange with other teams, you ensure that you have more data to draw insights from (and that your data is also used by other teams).

One company that does this well is Heineken. It is retrofitting its 173 breweries in more than 65 countries with digital capabilities on a single IoT platform. It created a proprietary data layer, scalable to include data from any source in a brewery. It extracts data from production facilities, normalizes it in a standard format, and makes it available to 17,000 workers on factory floors. They can apply it to use cases—what they see might be valuable in their brewery. Each use case is evaluated on KPIs plus user friendliness and operator satisfaction.[7]

Under current ways of doing business, one big roadblock to such good data flow is that most teams have people doing the wrong tasks. Ask yourself: how much time do your people spend on data collection versus communication versus decisions? For too many companies, the answers are something like 70%/20%/10%. This needs to be flipped on its head. Your people should spend most of their time on decisions plus a healthy chunk on communication. With good data flows and the new technologies, you can successfully free up resources to derive insights from data and make better decisions.

This is the flywheel. You collect data. You improve the quality of that data. You use the data to make decisions. You improve the decision-making process—and you discover the need for more data. The wheel has turned once. Now you collect more and improve more (a story we'll pick up in the next section, "Generate Additional Insights Through Connected Manufacturing"). Your algorithms get sharper, your people get smarter. It's hard work and seems to take forever. But if you can get the wheel spinning, its momentum will be unstoppable.

Knowledge is power, and data is now the fuel. The more data you have, the better you can quickly sense problems. You can get to the core of the problem, with richer perspectives to support wiser decisions. The faster the flywheel spins, the more you can use its energy.

In manufacturing, data analytics can help to visualize line down times and predict maintenance needs. In procurement, it can map supplier dependencies in tiers 2 and 3 and contribute to *should costing tools*. In logistics, it can unveil vulnerabilities by highlighting bottlenecks. In the warehouse, it can help optimize inventory levels (as discussed in Chapter 9 in the section, "Leverage Advanced Analytics in Customer Engagements Through Demand Sensing"). On the shop floor, it can visualize energy consumption and throughput per machine, comparing these KPIs to prior months in ways that help spot issues before they materialize. Financially, it can help balance capex and opex. In strategic planning, it can help assess, prioritize, and mitigate risks. Environmentally, it can measure, track, and model greenhouse gas emissions. With customers, it can speed your portfolio optimization projects (as discussed in Chapter 9 in the section, "Re-Engineer Your Product Portfolio Based on What Really Drives Customer Value"). In all of these uses, it's helping you combine efficiency with resilience.

## Generate Additional Insights Through Connected Manufacturing

A cow ingests an IoT sensor. The sensor starts communicating with the farmer. The signals give early warnings of infections and disease. The farmer can now figure out the best insemination windows and has advanced warning when the cow is about to give birth. In a world that has given us the Internet of Cows, imagine what sensors can do for your factory floor.[8]

Let's say that you've gotten your data in order. Your analytics team is deriving your first insights from that data. You are getting a better handle on the type of data that's interesting and valuable. And you realize that the good stuff isn't available. It's not measured. Time to buy some sensors and implement connected manufacturing!

The IoT can make your manufacturing more intelligent. Smart solutions can generate the additional data you need. This usually involves installing sensor technology on the shop floor, in the warehouse, and along transportation lanes.

Advanced technology can be interlinked to boost efficiency and resilience. For example, your existing security cameras could send a visual feed to an AI to make sure that everyone on the shop floor is wearing the required personal safety equipment. If part of the shop floor requires special equipment, a camera could monitor the door—and AI could lock it when someone approaches without the required equipment.

Sensors can provide valuable data at every step of a product's journey. Are there quality defects coming from the line? Are employees respecting social distance on the shop floor? Where is a specific shipping container, and how full is it?

You can start with a pilot project. To identify a use case, think about data you would like to have, how you could use it, and how that could help. Then discuss with your experts the needed technology (sensors? cameras?) and data analytics expertise. Then implement and review. Is the data helpful? Are you measuring the right things? What else can you do? If successful, you can start to roll out to more use cases and other production sites.

But remember that the goal is insights. Not data. You already have plenty of data—getting more won't necessarily help, unless you know how to use it. That means you need people who know how to use data, as well as people who know how to install sensors. Indeed, although some applications may require expensive high-definition cameras, much of your shop floor data can be collected by very simple sensors. And absent a semiconductor crisis, sensors are surprisingly cheap.

Instead, your biggest challenges will come from the data's relations to a wider world. Do you have a plan to harmonize data from different platforms? How about different factories, which may use different sensor technologies? Next, how do you integrate across operational and enterprise systems? Keep in mind that information technology and operational technology may have different priorities and architecture. You need to define data ownership and governance up front.[9]

But if you do so, the promise of connected manufacturing is that sensors can provide information that goes far beyond the data you traditionally generated. This data brings transparency. It thus helps to identify vulnerabilities and proactively mitigate risks. It can also help to significantly boost workplace safety and reduce accidents that lead to significant downtimes.

With such data, you can spot inefficiencies such as high energy use on a specific line. You can also be alerted to predictive maintenance needs. For example, if sensors show a machine vibrating more than it usually does, you can check to see if a screw is loose. Maintenance needs can be predicted by a variety of factors, such as vibration, heat generation, or noise generation. If you can combine all of these approaches, your AI can give you the warning weeks earlier than traditional methods.

## Share Data and Insights with Suppliers and Customers to Optimize End-to-End

The dog barks. The doorbell rings. As you walk toward your front door, you see your favorite delivery driver, who is scanning a package before leaving it on your doormat. As the driver turns to leave, as you open the door, as the dog's tail wags, your phone beeps. You have a text message, saying your package has been delivered. That's because the seller and shipper automatically share data with customers so that everyone can react to the same data simultaneously and in real time.[10]

If the seller is doing something similar with suppliers—and sharing insights as well as data—that seller is well on its way to optimizing its value chain for end-to-end resilience. As soon as you have improved data flow internally and established good data governance, it is time to extend the reach of your flywheel beyond your organization's boundaries. Sharing data with your suppliers and customers is an excellent way to find the best batch sizes, improve utilization, and reduce working capital. And all the while, you're generating value for the customer.

However, this is also a very tricky process. First, you need a high level of digital enablement and expertise. Second, you need that in your partners, too. Your suppliers and customers must be willing and able to engage with you in this way.

So find some key partners with whom you want to start this journey. These may be your strategic suppliers or your key accounts. Reach out to gauge their interest and capabilities. Do they want to do it? Can they even do it? As soon as these principal questions have been resolved, start to look into the technical feasibility. This is not an easy process. You will need to set up a cross-functional project team (IT, procurement, sales) that works closely with representatives from customers and suppliers.

When you seek to collaborate externally, the pitfalls of internal collaboration (discussed at the beginning of this chapter) get supersized. Your suppliers and customers likely have different systems. Linking them will be hard. Perfection will be impossible. Errors may proliferate. Delays may creep in—yet even a few days of delay render the data practically useless. That's why you want to start with a small number of key suppliers and customers first. Then take it step by step.

Likewise, your relationships with these external partners will be more complex than those with internal collaborators. You cannot force a supplier or customer to participate. If they aren't willing, you can try to do a lot of convincing—but the situation will also likely require a long-term change management process. You also have to be mindful of oversharing. Some of your suppliers might also deliver to your competitors, and you do not want your best-practice data to flow to the competition.

But again, the journey to resilience goes through transparency. Technology can give you transparency—about material flows, processes, and information flows—not only internally but also with your partners. For example, you can gain an early warning for supply or demand shocks. If your supplier is in trouble, you'll know in real time rather than whenever they decide to tell you. If demand for a particular product is cresting, you'll know in real time rather than after it's too late to avoid stock-outs.

Increased data sharing enables you to build resilience where it counts. Pandemic shortages demonstrated the need for safety stock of critical inputs. But it may be redundant for both you and a nearby supplier to invest in the same safety stocks. When you are sharing data, you are able to make your safety stock investments where they will reduce the most risk. (See the sidebar, "More Efficient Orthopedic Surgery.")

---

**MORE EFFICIENT ORTHOPEDIC SURGERY**

DePuy Synthes is the orthopedics company of Johnson & Johnson. Its products include artificial knees and hips. For such complex and expensive products, inefficiencies—such as high inventory levels and wasted time in the operating room—can really drive up costs. The inefficiencies can also reduce flexibility in times of disruption.

To address these concerns, DePuy Synthes linked its data with that of hospitals. Its advance case management (ACM) system uses patient data and procedure schedules to simplify pre-surgery processes. For example, automatic transfers of medical images streamline workflow in the office.

The integration effort faced many technical challenges to comply with legal restrictions for patient data. But real-time access to information such as X-rays and patient biometrics virtually eliminated time-consuming manual case coordination efforts. Furthermore, DePuy Synthes applies AI to that data (in addition to surgeon preferences) to predict the implant sizing range. In short, the AI, which learns from experience, is increasingly able to predict exactly which implant will be needed. Such predictions reduce inventory needs.

The AI can also predict which surgical instruments will be needed. This reduces the size of the surgeon's instrument tray. (Across surgical settings, a typical operation uses only 13 to 22% of instruments placed on surgical trays.) With fewer instruments to lay out and sterilize, the surgical team is able to reduce the time and waste associated with the surgery procedure.

With ACM, DePuy Synthes has halved its inventory footprint. It has reduced instrument tray needs by 63%—also reducing demand for sterilization equipment, plus the water, power, and materials used in sterilization.[11]

---

# Look Toward Automation to Build Resilient Operations

In the most famous sequence of the "I Love Lucy" TV show, the joke is that Lucy and Ethel have to be more resilient than an assembly line. Their job is to put wrappers on chocolate candies. But as the chocolates inexplicably arrive ever more quickly, they take increasingly extreme actions.[12] A lot has changed since the 1950s. (Indeed, other portions of the episode are cringe-inducing today.) Now automation can *improve* resilience, especially for such repetitive tasks.

As discussed in Chapter 5, cobots can take on jobs that require repetitive movements. For example, pick-and-place (moving a piece to a different location or orientation) is a simple and repetitive task good for cobots. So are packaging and palletizing (putting products into shrink-wrapping machines or onto pallets) and process tasks such as welding or gluing. Also valuable are *poka yoke* mechanisms—a Japanese term for "mistake-proofing" or "inadvertent error prevention." For example, an electric screwdriver might work only if placed on the correct screw as per the assembly manual. Poka yoke first came to prominence as a lean manufacturing ideal, but reducing errors is also good for resilience.

We're talking here about selected automation, not full automation. Full automation is usually too expensive; it can be brittle and fragile in the way of overextended supply lines; in most situations a common-sense human touch is still required. Other dangers of over-automatization include the following:

- Higher energy costs may detract from your sustainability goals or bring vulnerability to energy price spikes.
- You will need more maintenance. You're prone to equipment or power outages.
- Your demand for spare parts will increase. Are they loaded with semi-conductors, thus subjecting you to today's shortages? Or will some other small essential part headline tomorrow's shortages?
- You become more vulnerable to cyberattacks.

You need to find a mix of fully automated, semiautomated, and manual manufacturing in operations, depending on your industry.

To start, identify where you have the highest manual labor costs or the biggest risks to worker safety. Is it the assembly step? Grunt-worthy trench digging? Final packaging? How could automation assist these processes? As soon as you have identified what to do, talk to the people currently working the line to understand its nuances. These can be tender conversations—the line workers may be concerned that automation would steal their jobs. Be empathetic and share your plans for taking care of them as well as their functions.

Now make sure you've got the right visibility. You need to have the dataset that actually can drive automation. With a relatively complete dataset, you can draw insights. Insights become what software developers call *user stories*. User stories are what gets automated.[13]

As soon as you understand the potential in detail, do the business case. It's a long-term business case, because investments into automated production lines will play out over years, or even decades in some industries. It needs to account for hiccups such as power outages, energy price increases, or scarcity of spare parts. And ensure that you have the right people to support the process—don't pretend that you will eliminate labor costs. You still need technicians, engineers, and other essential people to enable the transformation (and that talent can be scarce).

By reducing your dependence on labor, automation can help to make you more resilient to shocks such as labor shortages, strikes, or pandemics. It ensures that you can more flexibly adapt capacity, and enables you to function with a smaller staff, which helps in times of a pandemic. By reducing manual mistakes, you cut waste and complexity. All of this builds resilient operations.

## Link Your Platforms, Globally and with External Partners

The most fascinating aspect of the race to build electric vehicles (EVs) is that the competitors are starting from totally opposite sides. Traditional automakers know how to build vehicles but have needed to learn about technology. Challengers such as Tesla and Rivian draw on many of the advantages of technology startups but have needed to learn how to make vehicles.

It's possible that both approaches will "win." But along the way, it's riveting to watch the startups set up a manufacturing environment from scratch. They can employ all of the latest analytics and AI. But they do so under heavy constraints in innovation and time to market—it's essential to basically invent all of the aspects of the EV, while also getting it done faster than competitors.

For example, Rivian needed to do a lot of crash testing and noise vibration testing on its new vehicles. But early in development, it didn't have a lot of extra physical vehicles to crash. So it sought to do real-world simulations using computer-aided engineering tools, which required a high-performance computing environment.

To do so, it migrated its software tools to Amazon Web Services (AWS), exploring the possibilities of high-performance computing in the cloud. Rivian chose AWS and the rest of its technology partners based on the mix of skill sets that it needed, and with confidence that AWS could mitigate the risks. Rivian was able to put all of the data from the vehicles themselves, the ERP system, and the manufacturing shop floor into a data lake on AWS.

It's a complicated partnership. Amazon is an investor in Rivian, and Rivian is building Amazon 100,000 exclusive cargo vehicles to be used for package deliveries. But clearly the technology portion of the partnership has helped Rivian link platforms and data companywide. As Rivian's innovative employees try to invent the EV, they are able to focus on innovations themselves rather than the technologies they use to innovate.[14]

The same may well hold for your company. Genuine innovation will come when you're able to link all of your global systems. The master class of digital enablement is to link everything you have cultivated in the prior four approaches into a single whole. How can the data generated and shared internally by different teams and functions—which is then extended by supplier and customer data and enriched by third-party service providers—be unified in a single data source? How do you ensure that the systems can be linked and that the data is comparable? Digital enablement—enabling this joint data foundation—is the key to unlocking the highest level of building resilience.

To link those systems—and to provide additional data—you'll need good partnerships. You don't have to do everything in-house. After all, your goal is constant learning. That is, you want to be constantly learning about how to solve your business challenges. Although important, your automation and AI challenges are in many cases too complex and too specific to insource. By identifying the right tech partners and data providers, you can improve your digital capabilities to support your business decisions.

The good news is that you have many potential partners to choose from. Particularly in recent years, the landscape of offerings and providers has expanded drastically. There is no need to reinvent the wheel internally when you can buy one from a tire store. But note that you never go into a tire store and think, "Wow, a sale on monster truck tires! Could I make them fit on my Prius?" Instead of identifying a partner and then thinking about how its solution can help you, you should first sit down to identify your pain points and needs. Then you can look around the market for a fitting solution. As soon as you have the use case identified, identify and start a joint pilot, optimally on the "best case" the partner focuses on. This way the partner will be demonstrating its best solution and gaining traction in your firm—because you can see if it works properly. You might ask for extra customer service for this pilot. If the pilot is a success, you can start to roll out.

But you're always starting by identifying the gaps in your current datasets and solutions. Are there ways to address those gaps internally at minimal investment? If yes, good. If not, talk to your existing tech partners. What can they offer or develop to address these problems?

Also talk to others. Do a market screening and request ideas and proposals from new firms. Review the offers you receive critically. Do they really address your core issues? Or are they standard solutions, quickly rehashed to appear to be tailored for you? Because every supply chain breaks in unique ways, you need to take time to identify partners that can offer a solution tailored to your problem. You probably want more than one partner—you're building an ecosystem—yet you also don't want to overextend it. Twenty different providers with point solutions is too many. Identify 5 to 10 that offer what you really need on an everyday basis.

As you look at data sources, be critical. How does the provider collect this data? Is it reliable? What bias could it have? How will it be anchored and used in your organization? Is the data available to everyone who needs it? Internally, data shouldn't be a well-guarded treasure—it should be used across the firm to drive value. It's never good to pay for services that add little value. It's worse when they *could* add value except that nobody uses them.

Now you can build a rudimentary system. Start enriching it with data. Be mindful of how the data you are adding relates to data that is already available. Slowly build up the system, bringing more and more data sources online. Continually test the system to make it better.

First you teach the system. Then you trust the system. This is not a blind trust, but a cooperative one. The system is a constantly learning technology. It learns from exceptions to optimize the road ahead.

The more data you link, the more complex questions it can answer. Early in your journey (as we discussed in the section, "Generate Additional Insights Through Connected Manufacturing"), you may only be able to test limited or simple hypotheses. Then you collect and connect more data. Eventually you go beyond your organization's boundaries, connecting to broader third-party data to derive more value.

For example, data from external providers can help you make environmental, safety, and governance decisions. Is your upstream supply chain relying on child labor or other exploitative practices? How much $CO_2$ is emitted? These and other potential weak points in your supply chain can be addressed by external sources, as we will discuss in Chapter 12.

Risk event data providers can identify supply chain disruptions and risk events in real time. These companies then calculate the expected business impacts of these events and the affected industries. If you're a client, you get a live alert to initiate mitigation efforts.

Other providers offer solutions that strengthen your internal resilience—the knowledge and flexibility you need to quickly respond to crises. For example, internal process mapping can identify where processes go awry and often break. Other technological tools, such as computer-aided engineering tools and digital twins, can augment your staff's ability to plan for and respond to differing scenarios.

CHAPTER 12

# Ensure Long-Term Resilience by Embracing Sustainability

To be resilient in the long run, you must grapple with sustainability issues. It can feel unpleasant, because people are always saying *you should, you must, you need to*. But if you can shut out the hectoring tone of voice, you may be able to see how initiatives such as *decarbonization* or *treating employees, contractors, and their communities with the respect they deserve* can make your operations more diverse and flexible. That can help you deal with the unexpected hurdles that a VUCA world will present. Here are five ways to start.

## Ensure Full Sustainability Compliance in Your Team and with Your Direct Partners

We firmly believe that sustainability is about more than complying with regulations. Investing in sustainability generates benefits far beyond the "not getting fined" part. When you do it right, it's a source of competitive advantage. As you seek to do it right, it's a mindset, it's a journey, it's a value to plant at the core of your firm.

But, hey, complying with all relevant regulations is a place to start.

And it turns out that this, too, is harder than it might sound, full of potentially conflicting stakeholders and targets. Regulations are changing quickly. Different countries, and even different US states, are taking different approaches and establishing different standards. Many organizations lack the data or capabilities to ensure that they are doing everything right—especially when there are so many different definitions of *right*. But the task is not impossible. It merely requires some diligence.

Teams should start to identify what they can do to ensure compliance in their department. This includes also establishing compliance with direct partners—mostly suppliers. After all, sustainability is always holistic. You can't be sustainable until your partners are. As you seek transparency with your internal and external partners, you should embrace diversity. As Chapter 10 discussed, the more diversity you have, the more resilient you'll be—by design.

Start by mapping the partners that make the biggest contributions to your sustainability impact. Maybe they burn a lot of carbon or maybe they operate in a place where nobody asks how much carbon they burn. Maybe they use a lot of low-wage labor and would be vulnerable to pressures to treat that labor unfairly. Does their supply base represent the diversity of the communities you serve? Reach out to them to start a discussion: How can we set joint goals, and then meet those goals? What are the legal frameworks that both of us need to comply with? How should we measure targets? How will we audit?

As soon as you and your partner(s) have some clarity, start to actively manage and document the compliance process. Then, after you have completed one wave of partners, extend these activities to the next wave. Then the next, and the next, until all of your direct partners are in compliance. Even then, you can't get complacent. Keep a watchful eye to ensure you stay compliant as legal frameworks change.

You may be tempted to limit yourself to emissions targets. Certainly it's important to reduce pollutants in highly regulated geographic areas. But sustainability is a complex construct encompassing environmental, social, and economic issues, and you need to engage it fully. For example, some unscrupulous players may try to push emissions and other harmful activities farther upstream. When it comes to emissions, scope 3 standards say that's not acceptable. But the principle applies to all sorts of ESG issues. They need to be solved, not hidden. This isn't three-card monte, it's the future of human society. Thus wherever possible your transparency efforts should go beyond your direct partners. You want compliance and transparency in tier 2 suppliers and ideally all the way back to raw materials suppliers.

Some people in your organization may view this as a *pro forma* exercise, simply checking boxes to follow an external edict. By contrast, make sure that your team sees value in the work. This is about your company working to build a better future.

A push to do this work may or may not come from the C-suite. Do it anyway. One reason: if you're the team lead who could have investigated a supplier's use of child labor—if it's *your* fault that the company suffers the high fines and public ignominy after the supplier's lapse is revealed—then who's going to tell the CEO all about it? We're betting it's going to be you, with resignation letter in hand.

The other big reason to do the work anyway is that you're not just doing it for legal reasons. You're doing it to build resilience. Resilience requires transparency into your processes and those of all your stakeholders—and so does the law. Transparency isn't just for regulators; it's helping you achieve flexibility in the face of supply and demand shocks.

Indeed, note that many potential "supply shocks" could be better classified as environmental, social, and governance (ESG) risks. For example, if one of your suppliers is using child labor and is found out, it will have to close. You will suddenly lose supply. And especially if you work for a large company, you may become the center of public controversy. It's better to gain the transparency internally and be able to act on it before it goes public. You gain more control, more flexibility, more resilience. It's always better to be proactively addressing all sorts of environmental and social problems and doing so in close alignment with your partners.

# Improve Self-Reliance Through Responsible Sourcing and Manufacturing Practices

As we discussed in Chapter 6, two productive ways to think about sustainability are in terms of *reducing waste* and *increasing diversity of thought*. Nobody likes waste. It's costly and inefficient. Reducing waste is a way to increase margins while also helping the environment. Likewise, almost everyone can see the value of solving problems with creative thinking and can acknowledge that diverse talent can increase such creative thinking. Here's how to implement those approaches.

Since the industrial revolution, the economy has operated on a linear "take-make-waste" basis, in which everything used by people ends up as waste. The most vital question of our age is how to prevent 100 billion tons of waste ending up in landfills every year.[1]

This is not a question of good and evil. The linear model brought millions of people out of poverty. And we've all participated. We've all thought, "I shouldn't waste this—but wait, *I'm* not paying for it! The *company* is paying for it!" And so we waste paper or office supplies or other materials, or we leave the lights or the heat on, wasting energy. In other words, moral scolding isn't the answer. But there *can* be productive responses. We can help everyone (including ourselves) appreciate how reducing waste benefits firm and environment. And we can set up the structures to make it happen on a scale beyond individual actions. In other words, we can think beyond the take-make-waste model.

There are lots of opportunities to look at things like sourcing and manufacturing processes. How can you redesign these processes to reduce waste? How can waste be reused or recycled?

Waste-based thinking can also apply to social dimensions. Think of the vast waste of intellectual resources that came about in the last century because of prejudice, when people of color were barred from certain professions or positions. Think of the waste of always building two separate drinking fountains, one for *whites only* and one for everyone else. Do vestiges of that thinking still afflict your processes? (And before you answer, "Heavens, no!", are you sure a person of color would answer the same way?) Where are you wasting opportunities by failing to leverage the diversity of your employees and suppliers?

Where is waste generated? You can map your material flows to find out. How much of the waste is necessary? You can do a critical review. That is to say, you'll bring in diverse perspectives (hello, diversity!). You'll encourage creativity. You'll think big, including product design. And you'll change the focus, from lowering costs to lowering impacts.

The diverse perspectives can also include customers and suppliers. Where do they generate waste? Do customers use the product as designed? Do suppliers take advantage of economies of scale? How could waste be reused or recycled? What would it take for such reuse or recycling to be efficient?

There are some pitfalls to avoid:

- In such a complex endeavor, you can easily find yourself going down rabbit-holes. Don't lose track of the big picture: focus on your biggest wastages and inefficiencies first.
- To achieve resilience, you likely have backup suppliers. As you implement waste reduction measures with your main supplier, you should probably also do the same with your alternate sources. If you don't, you may increase complexity.
- Don't assume that working with diverse suppliers is "charity": in other words, don't assume that you will have to sacrifice quality or pay more for goods and services. Diverse suppliers drive competition, offer innovation, and can often present more agile solutions.

It's worth negotiating these pitfalls because waste-based approaches almost always have bottom-line benefits. You can reduce your materials use, reduce your disposal costs, find new revenue streams from recycled products, and identify new revenue opportunities with diverse thinking.

When you reduce the number of materials you use (and waste), you reduce the risks of shortages in those materials. By recycling or reusing your waste, you are improving your self-reliance. Or if another company is paying you for stuff you once paid to take to the dump, you're increasing the resilience of your revenue streams. You're becoming more flexible. You may also be reducing complexity, which brings its own resilience benefits.

To illustrate, consider plastics. For decades, the US approach to plastic was largely "out of sight, out of mind." Plastic waste was shipped to China for recycling or disposal. Then, in 2017, China banned imported plastics. Southeast Asian countries followed suit. And the world discovered that many companies' value chains weren't very resilient when it came to disposing/recycling plastics. Some companies have responded admirably, reducing the amount of plastic in their packaging—aiming for *zero waste* rather than just exporting their problems to an allegedly distant corner of our solitary planet. But opportunities still abound. Indeed, plastic waste levels increased during the pandemic, while recycling waned. Later in this chapter, we'll examine possibilities for a regenerative, circular plastics economy. But for now our points are simpler. First, sometimes people don't see waste because of inertia and false assumptions (*We've always sent plastic to China—it's cheap because the ships are empty going back*). Second, eliminating this waste builds resilience against sudden changes in, say, Chinese import policies or ocean shipping patterns.[2]

Resilience is also about qualities of your firm and its relationship to its communities. Fair and socially just labor practices—within and outside of your company—ensure support from employees and suppliers during tough times. And if your employees and suppliers come from a strong community with effective safety nets, your firm is more resilient.

## Make Sustainability a Key Decision Metric in Your Business Cases

Consumers *know* how to make sustainable choices. In a Kearney Consumer Institute (KCI) survey, 85% said they generally knew how to shop sustainably for food, 84% for household products, 74% for clothing and footwear. But only 22% believed that these choices would have a large impact on sustainability outcomes.[3]

It's a catch-22: you want to make sustainable products, but you don't think consumers will care. Consumers want to care, but don't think you will make genuinely sustainable products. In Chapter 8 we argued that you can increase resilience by building trust across your supply chain. What if building trust with consumers could help build your long-term resilience? To do so, you need to fully embrace sustainability—as a key decision metric in all of your business cases.

When it comes to sustainability, we see most companies on a journey. First, compliance. Then, some individual, bottom-line-friendly sustainability initiatives. Then they sometimes falter. They've run out of projects with immediate favorable return on investment (ROI). They need to elevate sustainability in their business case approach. Sustainability needs to be addressed in conjunction with ROI, not as an afterthought.

This doesn't have to be mushy. You can and should define key sustainability metrics that matter to your business. One company came up with a universal measure (see the sidebar, "Merck's Companywide Sustainable Business Value Tool"). But you don't have to be that ambitious—you could pick a metric that's relevant to your industry. For example, for a manufacturer, the best metric for a business case might be carbon dioxide emissions. But an investment fund might want to look at the social impact of the investment. Likewise, metrics may differ by department or function. Procurement may be interested in carbon dioxide per unit, logistics in carbon dioxide per kilometer ton. Sales, meanwhile, may need to think about recycling rates.

---

### MERCK'S COMPANYWIDE SUSTAINABLE BUSINESS VALUE TOOL

Merck, the US pharmaceutical company, wanted a universal measure of sustainability impacts that could be translated into financial value. If Merck donates medicine to fight neglected tropical diseases, what's that worth? Would it be better to invest in programs to prevent diabetes? What's the environmental value of cell-based clean meat? Merck's many stakeholders—including investors, customers, employees, NGOs, media, and regulators—rely on the company to make smart decisions. It must maximize stakeholder value while ensuring financial performance.

*(continued)*

(*continued*)

So Merck developed a sustainable business value (SBV) tool to calculate and evaluate positive and negative impacts on the environment, society, and the economy. The tool collects different measures and assessments across Merck's value chain, including its suppliers, distributors, and consumers. It spans seven dimensions: environment, economic value, consumer well-being, digitization, ethics, governance, and societal enablement. Its quantification sometimes uses proxies, such as valuing a person's time based on national GDP per hour or valuing electricity based on the social cost of greenhouse gas emissions avoided.

Merck found that SBV estimates were informative exercises for management decisions and stakeholder interactions. Occasionally, compelling marketing narratives arose. SBV did not replace total shareholder returns (TSR), but an SBV-driven strategy could effectively augment TSR. The methodology behind SBV was recognized in the Assessment Concepts/Tool category at the 2021 German Award for Sustainability Projects.[4]

For each metric, define guidelines on how it needs to be measured. *Data governance* is an essential operational function because reliable sustainability data is essential to decision-making and accountability. For example PepsiCo, the US soft drink giant, publishes detailed information on its data processes, methodologies, and goals alongside all sustainability data.[5]

Then specify the minimum levels of these metrics that need to be reached in business cases. Make it mandatory. This is a simple alteration to your standard business case methodology. You're including a measure of sustainability, just like you can include other non-financial metrics. As long as the metrics are adhered to, you ensure that future projects have a given level of sustainability.

If you want to address the issue more broadly, with incentives, you could simply link executive pay to sustainability performance. (Then you can let *them* drive the methodology changes!) That's what Alcoa, the aluminum company, does. In 2020, 30% of its annual incentive compensation plan was linked to non-financial metrics in the environment, gender diversity, and health and safety.[6]

Note that all of this thinking applies equally to environmental issues or to diversity, equity, and inclusion (DEI) issues. You can recruit with intention to bring underrepresented groups into the fold. You can invest in quality DEI training. You can ensure that reduced office presence or flexible work hours do not limit employees' access to leadership, mentorship, and career opportunities. You can do all this not as an afterthought to ROI but as an equally ranking decision metric.[7]

You have to do all this because you believe in it. Because you're sincere—not because you're looking for customer validation. In other words: don't ask your customers to lead but accept that they are asking you to lead. As noted in the beginning of this section, KCI has found that customers know how to buy sustainably, but what they really want is trust. When you embrace sustainability, you are able to offer them products that they can trust will fit their needs. By contrast, KCI has found, when you merely embrace sustainability *marketing*, you risk sounding like you're virtue signaling or even greenwashing. That erodes customer trust.[8]

At this point in your sustainability journey, you're making more of a commitment, taking more of a leap of faith. You're doing so because companies with low investments in sustainability will lose competitive advantage and in the long run either be overtaken by more sustainable, innovative competitors or be thrown off track by more stringent regulations. Either way, they will fail to realize the commercial opportunities connected to engaging in sustainability.[9]

When you make sustainability part of the business case next to ROI, you choose projects that ensure long-term growth. You won't reject them in favor of short-term gain optimization (or even *lighthouse projects*, the initiatives that are admirably big picture but consciously small scale, and thus not a contributor to long-term growth unless adopted by the rest of the organization).

When your business cases have a long-term perspective, you ensure that they will also perform in changing market or business conditions. Furthermore, including sustainability in these considerations makes you more aware of associated sustainability risks. That will help you to prioritize projects that have lower risk, further building resilience.

# Define Quantifiable Sustainability Targets for Every Unit and Department

The previous approaches in this chapter have been somewhat tactical in that an individual business unit or project manager could implement them on a relatively small scale. But at some point you need to take a strategic approach. Your board and C-suite need to identify sustainability as a companywide goal.

To ensure a long-term, meaningful transformation toward more sustainability, you need to set clear and quantifiable targets. You're moving beyond the idea of having sustainability goals or considering sustainability in business cases. Now sustainability becomes proactive, something to plan for and orient on—a North Star.

But sustainability is complex. So you need to set targets at the unit and department level. How can each better orient to the North Star? How can each move the dial toward companywide targets? What can each start doing today? Different functions will have different requirements. But "every case is different" is not an excuse to let some cases off the hook. Every target must be oriented to the North Star. Every target must be quantifiable—specific and measurable. Every target must be achievable (although you may not yet know how). Every target must have clear responsibilities. Who is in charge of achieving it? What do they need to succeed? What happens if we fail? Presumably this is how other targets at your company work; sustainability is no different.

A target could be an $x$% reduction in carbon emissions for a plant or having $y$% of diverse suppliers. (DEI strategies are just like other strategies: you collect data, identify gaps, and make plans to close those gaps.[10]) The target could be more specific based on local operations. It could address water or other environmental issues, based on local needs.

Fit these targets into a road map. Allow for some leeway for changes in legal conditions, technology, or frameworks. But ensure that everyone on your team knows the road map. They should also know how they need to contribute to it.

Then you hold people accountable to those plans. Make sustainability target fulfilment part of feedback conversations. You might decide to link bonus incentives to achieving targets. You might even use a methodology, such as Kearney's Exponential Conversations, to evaluate board performance, uncover actionable opportunities, and address ongoing inequities in board membership.[11]

Remember, your broad ambition ("Net zero by 2040!") is only as good as your road map to get there. That's why you need to start today. The road map and today's goals are intertwined. You must succeed at both and then succeed at the actions to accomplish them. This is also why you need to set a healthy balance between a high-minded ambition and one that's achievable. You need to aim high to save the planet—but if your targets are nearly impossible, that will demoralize your teams and put stress on your organization.

You will face challenges in communicating this journey to the public. You want to avoid greenwashing—if you're going to talk the talk, you need to walk the walk. And remember that greenwashing is often a mere symptom of a broader failure of internal processes. It arises when your sustainability efforts are driven by marketers who are seeking to capitalize on consumer sentiments. Instead, the efforts should be driven by the C-suite, seeking to implement company values.

Public backlash against greenwashing can sometimes lead to *greenhushing*—deliberately not communicating your achievements. This is certainly a good way to avoid accusations of greenwashing. It's also a way to sidestep other criticisms, such as accusations that you're not doing enough. However, you don't want to let such fears totally dictate your public outreach strategies. In short, communication of targets is a key element of your sustainability quest, but it's a tricky line to maneuver.

How does a sound sustainability strategy lead to long-term resilience? There are two answers. Let's start with what we might call the *faith-based* approach. Many leaders today have faith that the future will require decarbonization and other environmental measures, will present challenges that can best be solved by diverse teams and suppliers, and will reward companies that drive sustainability into their core values. We call it *faith-based* not because it's religious but because it's hard to prove to the satisfaction of the entire world. Some leaders took a faith-based approach to capitalism in 1946, to globalization in 1989, and to vaccinations in 2020.

But if you're not yet willing to take a faith-based approach, you can take a *risk-based* approach. By ensuring you have a clear sustainability goal and all units and functions are aligned in working toward it, you will reduce your exposure to ESG risks, brand risks, risks of legal penalties, and so forth. You will also increase transparency, which will further boost your ability to withstand risks from pandemics, trade wars, natural disasters, and unforeseen crises. That's resilience.

## Close the Loop with Suppliers and Customers Through Circular Business Models

Even some members of our team thought *circularity* was a bit pie-in-the-sky. The whole point of business and commerce—of so many human endeavors—is to take stuff and transform it into something more useful. How could you do that while simultaneously retaining the same amount of original stuff?

Then they learned about PepsiCo's pledge to replenish more water than it consumes by 2030. Isn't Pepsi mostly water? (Not to mention Aquafina . . .) This sounds crazy! But PepsiCo is serious. It understands that some of the communities where it operates lack safe, clean water. It wants to improve water-use efficiency in its agricultural supply chain. It wants to inject water back into aquifers in high-stress areas. And it wants to work on conservation projects that make it easier for land to absorb rainwater.

Of course, making pledges is not the same as accomplishing goals. But it's notable how many large CPG companies are committing to water stewardship, among other sustainability projects. Indeed, PepsiCo is building on past successes: it doubled key water replenishment rates from 2016 to 2020. And when you think about it, in the biggest (global) picture, water is circular. Maybe it's worth working with that bigger picture rather than against it.[12]

Circularity is an extension of the approaches we discussed previously. We discussed reducing waste—circularity is zero waste.[13] We discussed working with suppliers to jointly adjust processes that improve efficiency—circularity closes that loop in terms of your material flows. Or maybe instead of closing a loop, you'll "cross" it: your waste byproduct becomes the input for another customer or supplier.

This is more about mindset than markets. For example, the circular operations of French footwear company Veja include using cotton grown with regenerative practices and repairing or recycling sneakers. Launching the repair program, cofounder Sébastien Kopp told *Vogue Business*, "You give a new life to what would go to trash. We are talking about making the product last 30 per cent more. It is magic for us. It has no price."[14] It sounds starry-eyed to the point of being out of touch with reality. Yet Veja's core proposition for customers is fashion and style rather than sustainability. The company is profitable because it believes in circularity but sells a total package.

Circularity is the master class of sustainability. It will not always be possible. But when you set it as an objective, your journey to reach it will provide benefits in sustainability, cost efficiency, and resilience. In the previous sections of this chapter, you found approaches to ensure compliance, improve self-reliance, greenlight specific projects, and achieve quantifiable targets. Now it's time to build on what you learned. How can you extend self-reliance to something more circular? How can individual projects build toward an ideal? How can your targets become more ambitious?[15]

To achieve simple sustainability goals, you probably moved beyond the scope of your company to address the entire supply chain. Now move beyond the scope of your supply chain! Would completely unrelated industries be interested in your waste? One person's trash is another's treasure, one person's meat is another's poison, one person's ceiling is another's floor, and so on. Maybe you're interested in someone else's waste! (See the sidebar, "The Circular Plastics Economy.")

## THE CIRCULAR PLASTICS ECONOMY

Despite the pile in your garage waiting to go to the recycling center, only 5% of global plastics are recycled.[16] Given its impact on the environment and human health, plastic has become a symbol of destructive waste. It's also a potential beacon for circular business models.

In Kearney's 2021 cross-industry circular economy study, more than 50% of companies reported setting circularity-specific targets—from using bio-based materials and designing products to be reused, recycled, or repaired to ensuring that products are made with recycled materials. For example, Coca-Cola aims to use at least 50% recycled material in its packaging by 2030, and Unilever plans to use 25% recycled plastic in its packaging by 2025.

Their biggest problem? Supply. Today, recycled feedstock supply is limited by less-than-ideal collection and sorting rates. Recycling is so small compared to landfilling that waste management companies have little incentive to invest in improvements. And technologies such as chemical recycling—which could turn plastic waste into valuable hydrogen—are still emerging. Kearney estimates that the US market could face as much as a 55% supply gap for recycled polyethylene terephthalate (PET) by 2030.

Solving the supply problem presents challenges. The world needs more and better recycling facilities, with better collection rates. But also, more products need to be designed to be recyclable. Commodities procurement experts need to wade through complicated cross-industry logistics. For example, recycled polyester used in apparel comes primarily from postconsumer PET bottle waste, requiring cross-industry collaboration. And there are lots of different types of plastics, with different potential recyclability, and different value chains to achieve that potential. Meanwhile, composite materials are virtually nonrecyclable. So if plastics are used in conjunction with other materials such as metal, paper, or wood, or with other plastics, they become difficult to separate.

The problem needs immediate attention. Companies with plastics in their value chains should understand the circular loop of each type of plastic, investigate nontraditional sources of supply, engage in partnerships to expand those supplies, and invest in emerging technologies. If they don't, they may struggle to meet their ESG goals.

At the same time, we find some small, heartening aspects to this challenge. First—like so many of today's challenges—it centers on resilience in operations. The challenges can be better solved by companies that have embraced the approaches described so far in this book: transparency, engagement, partnerships, technology, and operations excellence. For example, your DEI efforts may have included initiatives to make it easier to work with smaller companies. And suppliers of recycled materials are often smaller than suppliers of standard commodities, because they're specialized startups.

Second, the issue isn't the circularity mindset. Plastics recycling is embraced throughout the value chain, from the majority of consumers all the way to petrochemical companies such as ExxonMobil (which is partnering with Plastic Energy to pilot new ways to convert hard-to-recycle plastics into recycled raw materials). It's a lot easier to solve operational challenges when the incentives line up.[17]

When your operations are circular, you reduce material dependency. Your journey to achieve circularity boosts partnerships, transparency, and innovation across your value chain. Because you are following your product through the consumer use cycle, you're gaining insights into customer consumption patterns. And because you're doing the right thing for society, you strengthen employee retention and community relationships.

It's not easy. You may get stuck thinking about circular operations ("How am I going to collect those T-shirts/televisions/diamond rings from customers when they're done using them?"). If so, broaden the question to think about circular business models. How does your customer interact with your product? ("If they're just wearing the T-shirt once, maybe we rent it to them.") Would they be ready to bring it back to you to renew or refill it? ("Trade in your TV for a bigger screen!") Is a *transfer of ownership* really the best form of interaction between you and your customers? ("Under our subscription model, the diamond ring is yours at only a small fee for every month of marital bliss—and you can choose a totally different one for your next marriage." Hmmm, maybe not all business models work for all products.) When circularity gives you the privilege of interacting with your customers after the point of sale, are you ready to learn from them, upsell them, and/or build loyalty?

Your engineers will get excited about material flows. But you also want to think about holistic aspects of sustainability. At Kearney, rather than *circular*, we like to use the word *regenerative*. When your company is regenerative, it helps the community regenerate—by, for example, training talented employees in leadership and giving them the right work/life balance to exert those skills on the life side, too. When your company is regenerative, it helps the environment regenerate—by, for example, planting trees that improve the water retention rates of the surrounding soils.

PART III

# Outlook: Using Resilience Principles to Adapt to Future Scenarios

In Part I of this book, we laid out some strategies for achieving resilience. In Part II, we suggested some approaches to implement those strategies, complete with examples of how companies are doing so today. But will the strategies themselves be resilient? In other words, can you trust that they will be useful in the future?

In Part III we stress test the ideas of this book by watching them play out in various scenarios for the future. This also gives us a chance to see the strategies interacting with each other. And it gives you a chance to think about how you might implement them (or parts of them) in your own situation.

CHAPTER 13

# Potential Scenarios of the Future Economy

Nobody can predict the future. But we can describe some scenarios for how it might play out. Of course, there can be an endless number of scenarios depending on how detailed you want to get, but for the purposes of this book, we developed four.

## Laying Out Scenarios

To develop the scenarios, we identified the biggest questions that would shape the world between now and 2030—questions that could be answered in polar-opposite ways.

- **Resource availability.** Will we live in a **scarce** or **abundant** world? We're talking about *resources* in the tangible sense—materials, funding, technology, data—and also the intangible sense—favorable regulation, business opportunities. And although we ourselves cringe at the dehumanizing aspect of the characterization, we're also talking about resources in the form of labor. (As people ourselves, we know that any individual has far more to offer the world than merely laboring for a paycheck. At the same time, we have all been in situations where, compared to other situations, our and others' labor felt freer, more powerful, more creative, more abundant.)
- **Volatility of the business environment.** Will we live in a **stable** or **fast-changing** world? We're speaking not of *business volatility* (will the

stock market go up or down?) but volatility of the environments that businesses face. This includes politics, violent conflicts, public health, weather, civil unrest, and institutional erosion, among other conditions. The beginning of the 2020s marked an intensely volatile period. Will changes keep coming ever more quickly?

We considered several other issues that you always see in headlines, events and trends such as geopolitical instability, the cost of capital, the sustainability imperative, or the growth of AI. But we felt that these issues could all be handled in this framework. If these things happen quickly—sudden inflation, a surprise war, AI far ahead of predictions—the speed of that change will be a really big deal. And for a business, the implications of these issues are generally on resource availability: resources may be scarce because of inflation *or* recession, because of wars *or* environmental crises. For the purposes of imagining the world in 2030, these two axes cover a lot of ground (see Figure 13.1):

- In a **scarce** world, a general lack of critical resources reduces business and growth opportunities and causes a high level of competition between firms.
- In an **abundant** world, operations are not constrained by a lack of resources (nor are firms constrained by operations difficulties). As companies use operations to derive competitive advantage, resources are available.
- In a **fast-changing** world, we continue down the current path of erratic geopolitics, technological disruptions, and climate change–driven extreme weather effects.
- In a **stable** world, conflicts cool, relationships mend, climate progress is made, and disruptions are slow. In retrospect, the 1990s were surprisingly stable ("the end of history"), as were the 1950s—even though they followed the fast-changing eras of World War II and the fall of the Soviet Union.

Axes define quadrants, which here create our four scenarios (see Figure 13.2). We have named them long winter (scarce and stable),

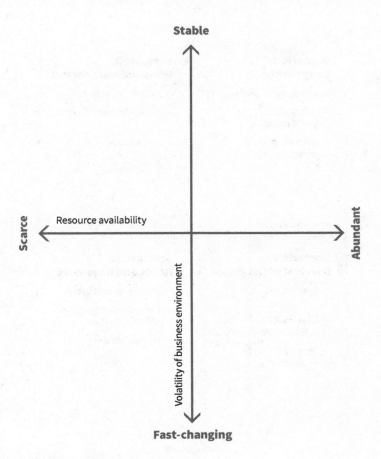

**Figure 13.1** Two axes of future scenarios
*Source:* Kearney analysis.

pre-pandemic normal (abundant and stable), survival of the fittest (scarce and fast changing), and haves and have-nots (abundant and fast changing). These are four cornerstones of the possible future. The actual future will not exactly resemble any one of these scenarios. It will be somewhere in the middle. But the purpose of establishing four cornerstones is to think about how a strategy would fare in each one of them—and thus how it would fare in wherever the future lands.

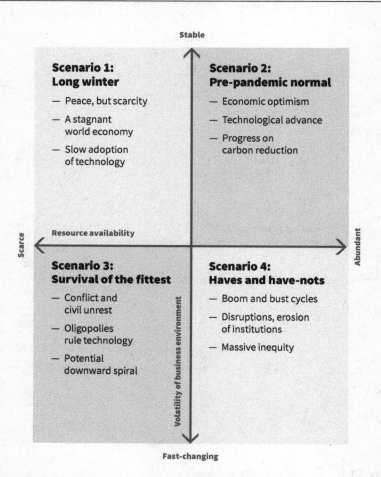

**Figure 13.2**    Four scenarios of the future
*Source:* Kearney analysis.

# Scenario 1: Long Winter

This scenario involves a long period of stability in which many people are tightening their belts. There aren't many resources to go around. That means companies with operations that can work within scarcity are set up to be comparatively more successful.

The long winter comes about because geopolitical conflicts subside but result in political/economic blocs. The tenuous peace limits economic freedom and access to raw materials and technology. The economic outlook varies by bloc: some blocs experience growth, but others shrink. The world economic outlook is stagnation, with a strong tendency toward protectionism and mercantilism. With decreases in global trade come decreases in overall purchasing power and wealth.

Generally, technological solutions are available, but their quality and adoption rates fluctuate. They're more available in some blocs than others. Competing national systems also cause a significant degree of parallel innovation, diverging technology, and de-standardization.

Likewise, there's variation in the degree to which companies and countries pursue sustainability efforts. Some blocs see incentives to forgo sustainability targets for short-term economic gain, which leads to a lack of global coordination. As a result, climate targets are missed.

Some disruptions continue, especially as extreme weather events rattle value chains. But with geopolitical conflicts cooling off, and technology changing slowly, massive disruptions are not a major concern.

Yet this scenario is where innovation really shines. The stable environment gives companies the safety to innovate. And innovation that replaces scarce resources offers great benefits.

## Scenario 2: Pre-Pandemic Normal

This scenario resembles pre-pandemic days, or the 1990s. Resources are abundant, and the pace of change is manageable. You can't erase the scars of the early 2020s—firms know how bad things can get in a pinch. They make contingency plans. But they have some confidence that those plans won't be needed.

Geopolitical conflicts cool off. Their resolutions keep global power dynamics basically intact. With relative peace, technological advancements, and an increase in circular business models, resources are generally available. The world is slowly mending. The overall optimistic outlook helps to build stability. There's no need for nostalgia for the pre-COVID days, because "normality" has returned.

The economic outlook involves cautious optimism. Economies recover from the early 2020s with small but stable growth. Inflation subsides to normal levels, and overall purchasing power increases.

Technological solutions become available around the globe. These diverse solutions include AI applications, plastics recycling, cheap low-carbon power, and cybersecurity. Although some traditional industries are disrupted, the net impact of technology is positive: economic recovery, growth in developing markets, control over cybercrime, and job opportunities to work with the new technologies.

In particular, tech advances boost sustainability efforts. Firms double down on their sustainability pledges. With global stability, they're willing and able to move toward joint industrial action. The cooperation and technology slowly move the global economy toward reducing emissions below the Paris Agreement targets.

Overall disruption levels decrease: no sudden invasions, no global riots, no pandemics. Smaller disruptions continue, of course—for example, surprise bottlenecks occasionally appear in supply chains—but companies are able to leverage their early-2020s expertise. They better anticipate and mitigate disruptions, further adding to stability and resource availability.

There's some pressure to innovate, because technology and data and know-how are all available, and you need to keep up. But with a return to the pre-pandemic normal comes a return to cost-focused operations. You gain competitive advantage through sustained operational excellence and economically viable use cases for change.

## Scenario 3: Survival of the Fittest

In this scenario, it's everyone for themselves. There aren't enough resources to go around, and yet the forms of scarcity—the threats—keep changing. Only those that are able to adapt and keep moving are able to stay viable.

Geopolitical tensions increase to extreme levels. Where 20th-century clashes were often about ideology, these represent intense competition for scarce resources. It's not just war, but civil unrest. Riots lead to further disruptions, further scarcities, and a downward spiral becomes difficult to escape.

A multiyear recession/depression causes significant GDP loss. Layoffs and bankruptcies cause high unemployment. Yet the cost of living increases, creating devastating poverty. Many markets experience a high level of merger and acquisition (M&A) activity as surviving players struggle to consolidate the power needed to ensure access to scarce resources.

Intellectual property (IP) protections dominate the dynamics of technology development. Transformative solutions are available only to a limited number of players. Challengers lack the resources to develop alternative solutions. Increasingly oligopolistic technology markets move toward a technocracy. As a result, end-to-end value chains face significant gaps in technology adoption, particularly in developing countries.

Amid the conflicts over rare resources, sustainability targets are continually downplayed, ignored, or even scorned. As a result, emissions and global warming far exceed the targets of the Paris Agreement. Yet this causes an acceleration in extreme weather effects, which only adds to the volatility.

Between geopolitical conflicts, civil unrest, climate emergencies, and poor progress on technology, disruptions are constant and extreme. With so few resources and so little trust, it's hard to build alternatives to fragile global value chains. Yet all the disruptions have significant implications on product availability. It's not just toilet paper shortages, it's food shortages—resulting in further civil unrest.

## Scenario 4: Haves and Have-Nots

This scenario is all about inequity. Resources are available, but the pace of change is too intense for slow-moving institutions to keep up with. Some players have learned how to anticipate and manage volatility, and thus thrive. Others have not.

Geopolitical conflict, climate change, and technological disruption lead to a highly volatile business environment. The good news is that resources are generally available, thanks to advances in technologies, circular business models, and data, along with thriving capital markets and favorable regulatory schemes. The bad news is that these advantages are poorly distributed. This results in massive inequity. Countries and firms with a talent for managing volatile conditions are able to claim a disproportionate share of resources for themselves. The untalented—or unlucky—get left behind.

Economies are unstable, with highly accelerated boom-and-bust cycles in specific geographies and industries. Instability leads to market consolidation and oligopolies. Governments can't pass laws fast enough to keep up with change; some are effectively captured by industries. Disproportionate resource allocation concentrates power in single players, which further erodes the effectiveness of institutional bodies, including industry associations and climate-change conclaves.

Technological solutions are generally available, but not everyone can implement them. In particular, developing markets and smaller firms lack the funds to close technological gaps in end-to-end value chains. Thus inequity accelerates.

Not all companies have sufficient resources to significantly invest into sustainability. The ones that do include sustainability specialist players and major players that are exposed to ESG pressures. Because of the fast pace of change—including rapid advances in circular business models and multi-local supply chains—these investments end up generating huge benefits. By contrast, the have-nots lack the organizational slack to invest into sustainability. So the net impact on global sustainability targets is determined by the level of inequity. The higher the inequity, the less likely that they will be reached.

The biggest inequities come in levels of disruption. Smaller, less agile, and less well-prepared companies face very high levels of disruption—economic, technological, competitive—driven by weather, war, and civil unrest. But the disruptions have less impact on major players and niche specialists because they have the right resource configuration to mitigate and endure.

## Scenarios and Strategies

Again, the point of developing scenarios is not to have a crystal ball. It's to have a framework from which to evaluate a strategy. We are *not* saying that the future will look like any of these scenarios. Instead, we're exploring the boundaries of the map of potential future outcomes. These four extreme cornerstone scenarios define that map. So if a company's strategy performs well in each of the four scenarios, that company is well prepared for whatever the future will hold.

In this book we have spelled out five principles that should guide your strategy as you seek resilience. Obviously, in a book for a general business audience, we can't lay out exactly how those principles will translate to a strategy for your company, your situation, your strengths and weaknesses, your culture. But we can show how the five principles might combine to drive competitive advantage in each of the four scenarios. Indeed, we can do so for four sample economic sectors. Chapter 14 takes a look.

CHAPTER 14

# Industry Case Studies on How the Principles Can Help in Future Scenarios

This chapter applies the ideas of this book across four sample economic sectors. For each industry, we'll first summarize key challenges and how firms can use our five principles to address them.

As we have consistently discussed, any given company will apply these principles in differing levels to their particular situations. This chapter shows how that might work: each industry discussion focuses on three of the five principles. That's not to say that the other two principles are useless for that economic sector, especially given how the principles overlap. Our goal is simply to show through industry-level analysis how you might use the principles to drive your own bespoke analysis.

Then we look at how those strategies play out for each industry across the four scenarios, providing resilience in a varied future.

## Pharmaceutical and Health Care Sector

Pharmaceutical and health care companies are all about patient well-being. Many of them thus have huge opportunities to place the

**customer** front and center. Indeed, to maintain their future product pipelines, they *must*: approximately 50% of the revenues of the 10 largest global pharmaceutical companies are at risk due to patent expiry through 2026.[1]

What do patients and medical professionals want and need? How can richer relationships smooth out operational challenges? Certainly the most recent industry crisis that required profound levels of resilience came on the demand side: the immense demand spikes related to COVID-19. In advance of the next potential spikes, leaders in this industry are increasing their use of advanced technologies to understand changing consumer behaviors and become better in sensing external demand shocks.

New treatments and technologies will also require customer-facing resilience. For example, three-dimensional printing of prostheses and artificial joints could give surgeons exactly what they're looking for, but this would completely disrupt traditional supply chains. In the long run, these disruptions should have positive impacts, including shorter waiting times for patients, personalized solutions, and lower working capital costs. But in the short term, quite a few players in this field would need to rethink their current operating and business models. Likewise, gene therapy is promising and personalized, but it has very high requirements for the cold chain. To be prepared, some companies are seeking to strengthen visibility, with a goal of quickly pivoting assets when channels shift. Some are building partnerships with specialized logistics providers that can ensure timely delivery at the right conditions for this high-maintenance, high-value cargo.

Many pharmaceutical companies are also facing huge challenges related to geographic supply risks. Although each company needs to map its individual supply base, in general, more than 80% of the key starting materials for active pharmaceutical ingredients (APIs) come from a single country in Asia. The industry is vulnerable to potential trade wars.[2]

**Technology** can help provide the required transparency and sensing solutions. Indeed, most leading pharmaceutical companies are improving real-time visibility across their logistics networks through solutions such as logistics control towers that digitize factories, distribution centers, and even all their machinery and vehicles. Some are also using AI to help with inventory management.

Some of the geographic risks are related to environmental concerns. Key starting materials for many APIs have negative environmental impacts, including emissions, soil acidification, and water pollution. As governments consider pulling home their pharmaceutical supply chains to reduce dependence on adversarial blocs, they risk increasing local environmental impacts. Thus as companies consider reshoring significant parts of their upstream operations, they should do so through a **sustainability** lens. Otherwise they will be met with a *not in my backyard* mindset in the markets they are reshoring to.

In the **long winter** scenario, pharmaceutical and health care firms face hard choices about R&D investments. On the one hand, future profitability depends on new products, and technology seems to be bringing us to the cusp of potential breakthroughs. On the other hand, a scarcity of resources could slash R&D budgets while technological developments stall. The key to success will be to get more out of existing resources. And, indeed, many pharma companies are already investing in AI for productivity improvements.[3]

Another concern is the input materials required. If critical input materials happen to come from a political bloc that has decided to impose trade restrictions, these companies face a nightmare. However, such conditions don't arise overnight. Companies that have pursued technology strategies will have better transparency across their value chains. Note that for this sector, the focus is more on politics than the fitness of suppliers themselves. Increased geopolitical tension between blocs—particularly on critical pharmaceutical goods—should cause policymakers to offer incentives to help firms become less dependent on foreign powers. That's the moment to switch from stockpiling to reshoring.

In the **pre-pandemic normal** scenario, long-term demand rises for geriatric care and related pharmaceuticals. The return to abundance causes life expectancies to increase around the globe. Pharmaceutical and health care firms can grow and innovate. They're not constrained by resource availability or economic instability. Expanding their product portfolio and tailoring it to specific markets will help firms to drive growth. Many players pursue scale through mergers and acquisitions; smaller and niche companies survive by staying close to their customers and even innovating in customer experience (as Hims and Hers are attempting).[4] Patient experience becomes the lever to drive integration across health care domains—we already see indications that players such as Kaiser Permanente have such ambitions.

In this scenario, firms are driven by sustainability concerns, both environmental and social. Some of the major challenges of the COVID days are being slowly resolved so customers and regulatory bodies are increasingly looking at climate change and social injustice. Their increasing demands for more sustainable solutions give an advantage to first movers who have implemented sustainability strategies.

In the **survival of the fittest** scenario, demand spikes. Pharmaceutical and health care companies struggle to meet it. Demand rises even above early-2020s levels because of the increase in disasters, civil unrest, disease outbreaks, and armed conflicts. However, resources to meet this demand are scarce. This scenario is hard on all industries but particularly challenging for pharmaceutical and health care firms.

To allocate their resources most effectively, companies need good visibility across global value chains. Those that have implemented technology approaches gain comparative advantage—especially when they use this technology to change business models, as Amazon is attempting with its RxPass offering. Benefits also accrue to companies that understand their customers, because they better know where the next demand spike might come from. Meanwhile, the high global disruption levels offer advantages to those that are as close to home markets as possible.

Even though few take sustainability seriously, the fraught political environment may cause tensions centered on negative environmental externalities. In other words, activists and regulators may still target the conditions of API production. Firms that have followed sustainability strategies know what it takes to be in compliance. They can effectively direct some of the limited resources to thereby avoid reputational damages.

In the **haves and have-nots** scenario, pharmaceutical and health care firms need to be fast and make bold moves. In an intensification of the winner-take-all markets they experienced in past decades, whichever company makes it first to market with a new drug can patent it and reap benefits for years. Second-place finishers have to write off significant R&D expenses. The issue isn't finding resources for R&D activity. The issue is how economic volatility and disruptions throw firms off track close to the finish line.

For example, if hospitals are tempted to stop clinical trials amid another disease outbreak, companies that have used customer strategies to work closely with hospitals may be able to call on those relationships. Likewise, companies that have implemented technology strategies will be better able to sense and react to similar crises. With risks so prevalent and unpredictable, risk management is essential. You need sophisticated risk management platforms that can sense events as they unfold and provide you with automated suggestions of mitigation actions to give you an edge over your competition.

Indeed, it can also be valuable to also see *integrated care* through the lens of risk management. How could a more integrated model of care delivery—such as pharmacies extending into clinical services—decrease costs without risking the service and quality expected of those footing the bill? A distinction between *haves* and *have-nots* may suggest differing models of value-based care, and firms need resilience in the face of these changes.[5]

## Technology Sector

Companies in the technology sector need to continue innovating and provide ever-new technological solutions for their customers. Thus future success arises from strong R&D capabilities, driven by the best **people.** Constant change and fierce competition mean that you need a good understanding of the **customer** base—what they want, and how and when. Because products can be complex, streamlining the product portfolio can generate significant benefits. Finally, you need the **technological** capabilities to make it happen. Data sharing is especially important for demand sensing, predictive quality assurance, and efficient logistics planning. Companies must communicate well to stay close to employees and customers.

The pandemic caused a demand spike for tech goods and services. Not every firm anticipated it. Yet first movers were able to significantly drive revenue and win market share. The companies that succeeded had often incorporated tools for continuous demand sensing and prediction. Other winning strategies included increased flexibility in logistics—with interchangeability in containers, machines, and digital systems along supply chains—and establishing consistent second sources with reduced geographic concentrations.[6]

In the **long winter** scenario, tech firms are forced to innovate because it's the only way to move themselves into a better resource position. They need better processes to conserve raw materials, a better brand to help in hiring, and better technologies to retain shares of smaller pies. Although conditions are tight, political stability allows for long-term planning to effectively deploy technology and people. Thus companies that have implemented strategies to develop diverse teams, extended learning curricula, and international expert exchanges are best poised for innovation-led growth.

Likewise, tech firms that started to implement the slow process of turning the analytics flywheel now see benefits. They're gaining insights—especially about customers—that competing firms don't have. And that's what distinguishes the winning innovations from the rest of the pack.

In the **pre-pandemic normal** scenario, tech firms can hope to see significant growth if they act quickly. General demand for technology shows a strong and healthy trajectory. Consumers have the disposable income to purchase electronics, and firms have the budget to further invest in digitization. Meanwhile, resources are generally available, so growth is not hampered by supply bottlenecks.

The question becomes, what's the best format? Advances in the metaverse or non-fungible tokens (NFTs) could offer opportunities to unlock new revenues through richer customer value propositions.[7] But beyond the technology, companies that have invested in customer strategies know what really drives customer value. In this industry, ena-bling product customization is a particularly valuable operational path to growth.

However, competition is fierce as competitors all try to capture as much of the market growth as they can for themselves. Companies suc-ceed when they have invested in technology and team strategies to build cutting-edge technology and employ the smartest minds in R&D.

In the **survival of the fittest** scenario, every firm struggles. Consumer demand lags as inflation eats into disposable income. Business demand also drops, because investments feel risky amid the many disruptions. B2B may be slightly more promising than B2C, because some players are making desperate, bold moves to retain relevance. But in general, tech firms that have implemented strategies to get as close to customers as possible can see the signs early and scale operations accordingly.

Due to the high volatility, teams are in constant firefighting mode. Companies that have built diverse teams gain the perspectives and resil-ience to solve unexpected problems. A joint purpose or vision aids people in enduring rather than walking away from adverse situations. Likewise, people who are well trained have the necessary mix of soft and hard skills to deal with crises as they unfold.

Tech companies that have implemented technology strategies are achieving transparency in operations. They're also taking advantage of capabilities in advanced planning, digital twinning, and scenario mod-eling. With these strengths, they can move quickly to make the most of the few opportunities that become available.

In the **haves and have-nots** scenario, the haves include tech firms that enable digitization and resilience for other firms. Many companies are seeking to safeguard their business from disruption by investing in digital platforms and tech solutions. B2B tech firms that are closer to their customers understand their needs and requirements and are able to profit from this trend. Those whose product portfolios lack solutions for resilience or digitization must instead find a small, specialized niche.

In the B2C sector, tech firms that are able to sense the change in their customer base can cater to the haves—the customer segments that have disposable income for consumption of consumer electronics.

Or, if they lack such high-margin, high-quality products, such customer-focused companies can use technology approaches to redesign based on cost. They make their products as cheap as possible to sell at smaller margins to the larger populations of have-nots.

## Manufacturing Sector

Manufacturing companies need to ensure that they strengthen their **supply** base. The semiconductor crisis, which affected all sorts of manufacturers, highlighted the risk of single-source dependencies and limited upstream transparency. Or, to put it more positively, the crisis highlighted the value of understanding semiconductor value chains and the interdependencies among them.

But it's not just semiconductors. For example, consider bicycles, where a pandemic-fueled surge in demand met massive shortages in components. Asian component suppliers had their output hindered by ongoing COVID-related lockdowns. Furthermore, their low-wage advantage was increasingly offset by higher transportation fees. It's an opportunity for nearshoring—but, more broadly, it's a classic example of the need to shift to resilient strategies. In short, to ensure component supply, all industrial companies need to identify suitable backup suppliers and strengthen strategic partnerships with key suppliers.[8]

**Technology** can help with transparency and inventory management to limit working capital costs. Data sharing and selective automation can optimize logistics and aid in planning for delays. Technology also helps to control the complexity that comes with dual sourcing and reshoring. Furthermore, as in the tech sector, manufacturing companies need to push the envelope on what is technologically possible in their product portfolio. A design-for-resilience approach—collaborating with suppliers to identify alternative materials and components—further builds flexibility where it counts.

To make this happen, industrial firms need the best **people:** engineers, developers, and technically proficient procurement professionals. The best approach to attract and retain this talent is to provide an attractive place to work. That effort can center on empowering the workforce:

providing employees with the opportunities and training to make smart decisions and perform well in a crisis.

In the **long winter** scenario, the scarcities of the pandemic only worsen. Fissures between geopolitical blocs heighten the dangers of single-source dependencies. Manufacturers have to invest in new sources (which is costly, though it has already begun) and/or fight for the finite available options (which is also costly). Thus companies that have implemented supply base resilience approaches have an advantage over companies that merely stockpiled critical inputs. They have already identified new potential suppliers. They have derisked their supplier portfolio geographically across tier 1 and tier 2 suppliers. They have identified new, alternative input materials and started to reshore or nearshore key inputs.

In an era of scarce resources, good people are a valuable resource. Talented engineers, developers, and managers are hard to come by. A company that understands its people and has encouraged them to find their purpose will have an advantage. Its leaders know why they are working and what makes them stay. So it holds on to them, even as competitors try to poach them. These people are thus able to drive innovation, including the highly complex R&D tasks involved in identifying alternative materials or reshoring. Those tasks—plus real-time insights from connected manufacturing—also benefit from implementation of technology.

In the **pre-pandemic normal** scenario, manufacturing companies should pursue an ambitious growth strategy. As they do so, companies that have worked closely with and empowered their supply base can leverage the boost in mutual understanding to innovate in product design and save money through joint process improvements. Likewise, companies that have implemented technology approaches can harvest insights from connected manufacturing and share those insights across a global manufacturing footprint or even with suppliers or customers. The two strategies combine to make these companies' growth initiatives more profitable than their competitors'.

With the ebb in constant firefighting, resources are available for R&D. Companies that have built resilient teams are closer to their people.

They're better able to let employees throw themselves into more visionary projects, defining their purpose and thus the company's purpose.

By contrast, the constant crises of the **survival of the fittest** scenario require continual firefighting. As in the long winter, combatting single-source dependencies is especially crucial. To be resilient amid myriad crises, manufacturing companies must trust their employees and suppliers. The companies that have empowered both their workforce and supply base will be able to build on pre-established trust to gain an advantage.

Diverse teams with rich training have the skills to handle these volatile situations. A critical supplier facing tough times is comfortable sharing data that provides early warning signs, and willing to accept help when needed. The decision to offer help is not an easy one (how critical *is* this supplier?). Nor are decisions about splitting orders among multiple suppliers to build secondary sources as backups—in tight times, these decisions can pressure the bottom line. But companies can enter the decision-making process confident that they understand the trade-offs between cost and resilience.

In the **haves and have-nots** scenario, the chief concern is power. Companies that already have an AI flywheel going can use data-driven insights in benchmarking studies to see if they have a chance to become an undisputed leader in their area. If so, resources are available to make that power play. If not, companies can identify and defend a niche.

Defining that niche—perhaps by geographic market or by product solution—also relies on technology, including data that is linked globally and with external partners. To defend the niche, companies that are close to their suppliers can become preferred customers. With transparency and collaborative optimization, they build resilience against forays by competitors and against the frequent supply and demand shocks that plague the economy.

## Retail and Consumer Goods Sector

A traditional strength of retailers and consumer packaged goods (CPG) companies has always been their proximity to **end consumers**.

They can build resilience by continuing to expand that intimacy. As consumer demand changes, they need to know how and understand why. They also need to be able to ripple those changes back through the value chain to react quickly. Most of this book's examples of design-to-value and product portfolio optimization (in Chapter 3, sections "Know What Drives Customer Value" and "Drive Out Complexity," and in Chapter 9, section "Re-Engineer Your Product Portfolio Based on What Really Drives Customer Value") apply here. Likewise, consumers increasingly desire omnichannel fulfillment, and leading firms engage in design processes and scenario planning to meet those needs.

Thus these companies also need to work closely with **suppliers** to jointly create value. Digital connectivity can lead to increased flexibility and agility to meet those changing consumer demands. Close collaboration with logistics suppliers will speed that reaction time to changing consumer demands. And with last-mile logistics such a competitive and fast-changing sector, smart strategies and deep collaborations can build resilience to unexpected developments.[9]

For many products, consumer preferences are evolving toward **sustainability**: in the product, the transport, the packaging, and more. Thus CPG and retail firms should work closely with their upstream network to gain transparency on carbon footprints and labor conditions. Although some firms will merely pay lip service to sustainability ideals, those who engage in design-for-sustainability efforts will reap larger benefits.

In the **long winter** scenario, demand is low. To profit, companies must generate the highest possible margin on every sale and capture the highest possible share of the market. Companies that are close to their customers can invest scarce resources in areas that will create the most value. They can be confident about these decisions because they understand their customers' needs. They are able to redesign products and simplify portfolios to save money without losing sales.

Meanwhile, companies that have implemented supplier and sustainability strategies can work with suppliers to reduce waste, yielding environmental benefits plus cost reductions in a low-margin environment. They can conduct supplier fitness programs to support key suppliers in times of need. And their knowledge of sustainability issues can prove useful if standards evolve differently in different blocs.

In the **pre-pandemic normal** scenario, growth markets exist—the key is to find them. Companies that are operating for their customers can do so with demand sensing and frequent customer feedback. They are tailoring their products to customer desires. Sustainable products will probably be one of the key growth markets. Companies that have embraced sustainability in operations can better capture those markets with a strong brand and authentic commitment.

Meanwhile, companies that have empowered their supply base are able to work closely with those suppliers to create innovations in products and how they are used. Resources are available, so these companies can also work with suppliers and customers to identify innovative new circular operating and business models.

In the **survival of the fittest** scenario, retail and CPG firms face continual threats from external crises such as bans of food exports or big price hikes for ingredients. Consumers are spending less, and food markets are particularly affected by fertilizer shortages. Are companies ready to change their plans? Can they move fast enough to survive?

Those that have implemented customer strategies can ensure first-mover advantages through demand sensing. They also have advanced warning about declining markets and products. Meanwhile, companies that have established upstream supply visibility can identify crises, be they supplier bankruptcies or societal shifts. Finally, companies that have invested in sustainability have increased their self-reliance to make resources last longer.

In the **haves and have-nots** scenario, retail firms are especially concerned about external shocks limiting continued access to resources amid volatility. Companies that are close to their suppliers and customers are best positioned to build multi-local supply chains, in the region, for the region. They reduce reliance on global supply chains that are more easily disrupted by weather effects, congestions, or conflicts, while also staying closer to their consumers.

Consumer preferences shift rapidly, so these companies are also better able to innovate—including in sustainability. With upstream visibility and even some management of tier 2 suppliers, they reduce risks of supply disruption. And with deep customer understanding, they're able to move into newer, less contested segments. They can even think about new business models such as renting rather than purchasing luxury goods.

CHAPTER 15

# Common Themes
# We See in All
# Transformations

The future won't look like any of the scenarios we've laid out for any of the industries we've examined. It will be some unexpected combination of those factors, which will apply differently to every industry and firm. But the exercise of working through the scenarios helps stress test the strategies. From those tests emerge some themes common to all industries.

One theme is *transparency and visibility*. Resilience is about being able to react more quickly. The more upstream visibility you have into your supply chain, the more quickly you can react. It doesn't matter whether you're reacting to volatility or stability, to abundance or scarcity—or whether your reaction takes the form of changing designs or specifications, increasing outputs, enhancing sustainability, supporting suppliers, or changing suppliers amid a reshoring effort. The first step is being able to see what's currently going on.

A second theme is *data*. Today's world is full of data, but the key to success is sharing it in useful forms. The more you know, the better decisions you can make. Again, that's true regardless of what those decisions are or what conditions they're responding to. Data is a component of the transparency previously discussed (though the transparency also requires relationship building). But data is also what drives insights into customers, internal processes, and wise investments.

Third, operations leaders should always think about *generating value for customers*. This may seem obvious, but too often in the past, it's been obscured by the importance placed on thinking about costs. Sometimes value does take the form of lowest cost—but it can take many other forms as well. Sometimes sustainability is more costly, but customers value it. Sometimes reshoring is more costly in some ways, but less so in others. Sometimes resilience is more costly, but you create value by guaranteeing that you can come through in a crisis.

A fourth theme is one we like to summarize as *challenge*. Resilience benefits from challenging your product and its specifications. How do you source it? How do you manufacture it? How do your customers use it? The theme of the world today is change, and that means that your products and operations must change, too. So why not be proactive? Why not challenge yourself? For example, one challenge is to ask, *How can we do this more sustainably?* If you suspect that customer sentiments and/or regulations are changing, now is the time to get your surfboards ready for the wave rather than be swamped under it.

Finally, technology is an excellent tool—but *supply chains are mostly about people*. To draw benefits from the best technology, you need the right people. To attract and retain the right people, you need to create an environment where they want to work. And to make sure they have the right purposes and motivations, you need to trust and empower them.

# CHAPTER 16

# Some Questions to Ask Yourself About the Future of Your Operations

Reading this book should not be a theoretical exercise or a thought experiment. Instead, it should be a conversation starter. We want you to be able to use it to begin solving your own specific problems. We believe that such solutions will lead—maybe now, maybe later, depending on the dynamics of your situation—to a rich and productive transformation of your entire enterprise.

Transformations are good. Indeed they're required, because that's how the VUCA world works. Sooner or later, the need to transform will present itself. You will be asked questions, maybe as soon as tomorrow. To be prepared, you might want to start thinking about the answers today.

Some of these questions may include the following:

*How will your business model change?* For example, as the world presents opportunities to get closer to your customers, or move toward circularity, will you be better off changing the parameters by which you make money? The profitable innovation in the fast-fashion industry wasn't just making clothes more quickly, it was changing the business model to take advantage of that.

*Will you take advantage of new customer segments or geographies?* We tend to see volatility as bad because it destroys existing ways of doing business. Whether it's hurricanes, wars, or changes in fickle consumer sentiments, we wish for the simplicity of stability. But as Joseph Schumpeter said, the magic of capitalism is *creative destruction*, and thus the most magical players are always dynamic. How can you take advantage of a newly volatile world?

*What happens to your products?* In a newly digital world, are there better ways to make your products? Can you design them more collaboratively? If disruptions create physical barriers in your global supply chains, how do you respond?

*How can you change your measurements?* For example, consumers increasingly value measures of recyclability. Can you provide those measurements? And in an omnichannel world, practices that make sense for one channel (such as oversized packaging to reduce theft in retail settings) seem silly in a different channel (such as online, where the oversized packaging needlessly increases distribution costs). You reduce such inefficiencies only when they're measured—but how?

*Do you need new cooperative models?* Our complex world involves increasing profiles for non-shareholder stakeholders in your company— suppliers, partners, employees, governments, and even sometimes competitors. Would you be more resilient if you moved toward more cooperation with them? And if you moved toward more formalized models for cooperations? For example, in 2022, Intel and Brookfield Asset Management responded to the semiconductor crisis by signing a $30 billion deal to build semiconductor factories in Arizona. The innovative approach to funding growth in a fast-changing sector relied on a new form of cooperative model.[1]

*Do you have the right operating model?* When the world becomes more complex, you often need to simplify your operating model—the processes, structures, and unwritten rules that govern how you get things done. Externally, complexity is a fact of life. Internally, complexity can make you too slow, too rigid, or too expensive. Could you optimize your organization's culture and ways of working?[2] To do so, you can start with tiny steps. See the sidebar, "The Smaller Questions."

---

### THE SMALLER QUESTIONS

Collaboration has been a big theme of this book, and as we collaborated in authoring it, we found that we had different approaches. Some of us gravitate toward the big questions: *what does this imply about, say, operating models?* And some of us gravitate toward smaller questions: *what's a task that a reader can embark on today and hope to finish soon?* Here are some such smaller questions.

- Where are your supplier risk hot spots? Could you ask your teams to assess supplier segmentation by category, identifying single-source, geographic, and other risks?
- Could you meet with the CEO of a key supplier? An early step in collaboration is to invite them for a strategy meeting.
- What words do people use to talk about your company? Could your social media team find out by data mining all mentions of your company name in Twitter, Instagram, and other platforms?
- What's important to your key customers? If you're a B2B business, could you invite those customers for a strategy meeting? If you're B2C, could you host a consumer-sharing session?
- Do your employees understand the state of your firm and its strategic direction? Is now a good time to host an all-employee townhall meeting to update them?
- When was the last time an employee told you something you didn't want to hear (but needed to hear)? Might you host an anonymous employee survey full of provocative questions that could lead to such insights?
- Can you study a map of your digital ecosystem? What companies are you working with, and what services are they offering? What gaps do you see?
- What does your data team need to start an analytics/AI flywheel? (If you don't have a data team, do you need to start by founding one?)
- Where are your sustainability gaps, and how can you address them? The best place to start may be by reading your own sustainability report.
- Where do you fit on Kearney's Sustainability Chessboard? What does that imply about your next move?[3]

Throughout this book, we've tried to provide answers: answers to what resilience is, and what it requires. Answers to how to think about your supply base, where you can anticipate customer needs, why to reconsider your employee value proposition, how to build an AI/analytics flywheel, and why sustainability matters (or *should* matter now because it *will* matter soon). Yet after all that, now we're leaving you with questions.

Because that's how transformations work. That's how wisdom works. Socrates was the wisest person in Athens but believed that he knew nothing—his relative wisdom came only from recognizing his own ignorance. Or, in the words of Yoda from *Star Wars*, "Always more questions than answers, there are."[4]

Questions define the route to transformation. We hope that, if your company does end up embarking on a transformation journey, you find it as fulfilling as our company's journey is for us.

# NOTES

## Preface  Building Strong Supply Chains to Profit Despite Disruptions

1. The term VUCA originated with the US Army War College, describing military strategy in a post–Cold War world. See https://usawc.libanswers.com/faq/84869, accessed December 6, 2022.
2. For the story of Kearney, see https://www.kearney.com/about-kearney/our-story, accessed December 3, 2022.

## Chapter 1  Strong Operations Drive Growth and Profits by Adjusting to an Ever-Changing World

1. For the original Lean principles, see Jeffrey Liker, *The Toyota Way: 14 Management Principles from the World's Greatest Manufacturer* (New York: McGraw Hill, 2020).
2. For more on the Kearney COO survey, see Suketu Gandhi, Michael F. Strohmer, Marc Lakner, and Tom Adams, "Optimism in Operations: Why COOs Are the Key to Corporate Regeneration," https://www.kearney.com/operations-performance-transformation/article/-/insights/optimism-in-operations-why-coos-are-the-key-to-corporate-regeneration, March 1, 2023.
3. For a full summary of risks, see the World Economic Forum, *The Global Risks Report 2022, 17th Edition* (Geneva, Switzerland: World Economic Forum, 2022).
4. For more on Sense and Pivot, see https://www.kearney.com/operations-performance-transformation/resilient-supply-chains, accessed December 21, 2022.
5. For more on the Resilience Stress Test, see *MIT Technology Review Insights*, "Building Resilient Supply Chains," https://mittrinsights.s3.amazonaws.com/SupplyChain.pdf, accessed December 21, 2022; Charisse Jacques, "Strategic Options to Build Resilience," https://www.kearney.com/operations-performance-transformation/article/-/insights/strategic-options-to-build-resilience, accessed December 21, 2022.

6. For the value of focusing on weak spots, see Steve Mehltretter, James Harford, and Subhash Shanmugasundaram, "Build a Robust Supply Chain by Putting a Spotlight on the Weak Spots," https://www.kearney.com/operations-performance-transformation/article/-/insights/build-a-robust-supply-chain-by-putting-a-spotlight-on-the-weak-spots, March 3, 2021.

7. For a history of reshoring, see the annual Kearney US Reshoring Index, published by the Kearney Supply Chain Institute (KSCI), https://www.kearney.com/operations-performance-transformation/us-reshoring-index. Note, however, that reshoring decisions are equally important outside the US. As we will see in Chapter 9, even lower-cost countries can benefit from companies operating "in the region, for the region."

8. For Warby Parker and more, see Laurent Chevreux, Michael Hu, and Suketu Gandhi, "Why Supply Chains Must Pivot," *MIT Sloan Management Review* (July 19, 2018), https://sloanreview.mit.edu/article/why-supply-chains-must-pivot/. For pharmaceutical pivots, see "The Future of Pharma: Three Critical Steps Toward Creating a Pivoting Supply Chain," https://www.kearney.com/health/pivoting-pharma-supply-chains-in-a-digital-world/article/-/insights/the-future-of-pharma-three-critical-steps-toward-creating-a-pivoting-supply-chain, October 21, 2019.

# Chapter 2  Principle 1

1. For effects of the automobile semiconductor shortage, see, for example, Michael Wayland, "Ford Reports Smaller Sales Decline in April While Chip Shortage Weighs on Supply," CNBC (May 4, 2022); "Cox Automotive Lowers Full-Year New-Vehicle Sales Forecast as Persistent Supply Problems Continue to Hold Back Auto Industry" (June 28, 2022), https://www.coxautoinc.com/news/cox-automotive-lowers-full-year-new-vehicle-sales-forecast-as-persistent-supply-problems-continue-to-hold-back-auto-industry/; Alisa Priddle, "Ford Cuts F-150 Production Due to Semiconductor Chip Shortage," *Motortrend* (February 5, 2021).

2. For more on semiconductors and automakers, see Mike Hales, Danish Faruqui, Dieter Gerdemann, Bharat Kapoor, Hieu Pham, and Archit Johar, "Why a Resilient Semiconductor Supply Chain Is Imperative—and How to Create One," https://www.kearney.com/technology/article/-/insights/why-a-resilient-semiconductor-supply-chain-is-imperative-and-how-to-create-one, May 11, 2021; Dieter Gerdemann, Guido Hertel, Thomas Luk, and Michael F. Strohmer, "Alleviating the Urgent Need for Semiconductors," https://www.kearney.com/technology/article/-/insights/alleviating-the-urgent-need-for-semiconductors, February 22, 2021; Cary Shiao, Bharat Kapoor, Dieter Gerdemann, and Guido Hertel, "Automotive Semiconductor Supply: Looking Beyond Yesterday," https://www.kearney.com/technology/article/-/insights/automotive-semiconductor-supply-looking-beyond-yesterday, March 24, 2021.

3. For more on Toyota and semiconductors, see River Davis, "Supply-Chain Savvy Spared Toyota from the Global Chip Crisis," *Bloomberg News* (April 7, 2021); "Carmakers to Suffer Chip Shortages Until at Least End of 2023," *Financial Times* (December 19, 2022).

4. For a full treatment of SRM, see Mike Hales, Michael F. Strohmer et al., *Supplier Relationship Management: How to Maximize Vendor Value and Opportunity* (New York: Apress, 2014) or the summary "Supplier Excellence" at https://www.kearney.com/article/-/insights/supplier-excellence-procurement-capability-article, accessed January 3, 2023.

5. For more on disruptive procurement, see Michael F. Strohmer, "Disruptive Procurement: Reinventing and Transforming the Procurement Function," https://www.kearney.com/procurement/article/-/insights/disruptive-procurement-reinventing-and-transforming-the-procurement-function, January 5, 2020.

6. For more on complex supply networks, see Per Kristian Hong, Nigel Pekenc, and Xavier Mesnard, "How Can We Achieve Resilient, Net-Zero Global Value Chains? A Summary of Discussions from the World Economic Forum Annual Meeting," https://www.kearney.com/global-strategic-partnerships/world-economic-forum/article/-/insights/how-can-we-achieve-resilient-net-zero-global-value-chains, July 26, 2022.

7. For details on what to reshore first, see Suketu Gandhi, "Leveraging New Tech to Boost Supply Chain Resilience," *Harvard Business Review* (October 26, 2022), https://hbr.org/2022/10/leveraging-new-tech-to-boost-supply-chain-resilience.

8. For more on reshoring strategy, see Marc Lakner, Suketu Gandhi, Sherri He, and Philip Wessely, "The Reshoring Revolution: When to Reshore in a New Global Economy," https://www.kearney.com/operations-performance-transformation/article/-/insights/the-reshoring-revolution-when-to-reshore-in-a-new-global-economy, July 25, 2022.

9. For more on the unchained future, see Suketu Gandhi and Saad Farhard, "Will Supply Chain Tech Be Bigger than Fintech?" https://www.kearney.com/operations-performance-transformation/article/-/insights/will-supply-chain-tech-be-bigger-than-fintech, October 18, 2022.

# Chapter 3   Principle 2

1. For more on the apparel industry, see Pei Yun Teng, "Social Innovation Offers Five Golden Opportunities to the Apparel Industry," https://www.kearney.com/why-us/social-impact-and-sustainability/article/-/insights/social-innovation-offers-five-golden-opportunities-to-the-apparel-industry-article, November 8, 2017.

2. Donald Sull and Stefano Turconi, "Fast Fashion Lessons," *Business Strategy Review* 19, no. 2 (2008): 4–11. https://doi.org/10.1111/j.1467-8616.2008.00527.x.

3. Rachel Monroe, "Ultra-fast Fashion Is Eating the World," *The Atlantic* (March 2021).

4. For more on direct-to-consumer strategies, see Rhiannon Thomas, Eric Gervet, Thibault Hollinger, and Guillaume Bochu, "Building Brands Through Online D2C," https://www.kearney.com/consumer-retail/article/-/insights/building-brands-through-online-d2c, March 7, 2023.

5. For more on design-to-value, see Greg Portell, Arun Kochar, and Jesse Chafin, "Elevated, Agile, and Crowdsourced Design-to-Value Reaps Financial and Sustainability Gains," https://www.kearney.com/operations-performance-transformation/article/-/insights/elevated-agile-and-crowdsourced-design-to-value-reaps-financial-and-sustainability-gains, August 11, 2021.

6. For more on SKU optimization, see Marybeth Hays and Steve Cunix, "Merchandising in the No Normal—What Now?" https://www.kearney.com/consumer-retail/merchandising-in-the-no-normal-what-now, accessed January 11, 2023.

7. For more on platforming, including Lego and Helix Sleep, see Bharat Kapoor, Brent Ross, Kushal Fernandes, and Alexander Bruns, "Platforming: The Best Solution to Product Line Complexity," https://www.kearney.com/operations-performance-transformation/article/-/insights/platforming-the-best-solution-to-product-line-complexity, March 1, 2021.

8. For more on how to simplify your portfolio, see Moritz Tybus and Gian Carlo Bauer, "Product Portfolio Simplification," https://www.kearney.com/communications-media-technology/article/-/insights/product-portfolio-simplification, September 2, 2020.

9. For more on retail calendars, see Michael Brown and Greg Portell, "Traditional Retail Calendars and Staffing Models: Casualties of the No Normal," https://www.kearney.com/consumer-retail/article/-/insights/traditional-retail-calendars-and-staffing-models-casualties-of-the-no-normal, July 23, 2020; Hays and Cunix, "Merchandising in the No Normal—What Now?"

10. For more on consumers' varying perceptions of quality, see Katie Thomas and Tanya Moryoussef, "The Death of Price/Value and Dissection of Quality," https://www.kearney.com/consumer-retail/article/-/insights/the-death-of-price-value-and-dissection-of-quality, August 16, 2022.

11. For more on consumers and convenience, see Katie Thomas, "Deconstructing Consumer Convenience," https://www.kearney.com/consumer-retail/article/-/insights/easy-like-sunday-morning-kci-quarterly-briefing-q3-2021, August 13, 2021.

12. For more on supply chain planning, see Suketu Gandhi, Nikhil Mishra, and Erin Chiang, "Stop Looking in All the Wrong Places for Supply Chain Solutions—and Start with Planning," https://www.kearney.com/operations-performance-transformation/article/-/insights/stop-looking-in-all-the-wrong-places-for-supply-chain-solutions-and-start-with-planning, November 9, 2022.

13. For more on shape of demand, see Sameer Anand, Adheer Bahulkar, and Aman Husain, "What Got Us Here Will Not Get Us There," *Supply Chain*

*Management Review* (January/February 2021), https://www.kearney.com/documents/291362523/291370161/SCMR2101_C_Ops_Adv.pdf/26a8e22f-f7ea-ca5a-cfdf-3f3389458951?t=1612948448000.

14. For more on Janus by Kearney, a custom demand intelligence capability, see Sameer Anand and Adheer Bahulkar, "Navigating the Shape of Demand," https://www.kearney.com/operations-performance-transformation/article/-/insights/navigating-the-shape-of-demand, September 6, 2021.

15. Our point is about resilience in the immediate responses to the pandemic-fueled last-mile crisis. The last-mile/first-mile segment has since become far more sophisticated; see Balika Sonthalia, Rupal Deshmukh, Marc Palazzolo, and Elise Kerner, "How Can Retailers Build Resilience in Last-Mile Distribution?" https://www.kearney.com/telecommunications/article/-/insights/how-can-retailers-build-resilience-in-last-mile-distribution, December 21, 2021; Balika Sonthalia, Anna Kraft, Marc Palazzolo, and Abi Osunsanya, "Solving Tech's Last-Mile/First-Mile Problem," https://www.kearney.com/operations-performance-transformation/article/-/insights/solving-techs-last-mile-first-mile-problem, August 15, 2022.

# Chapter 4 Principle 3

1. For more on CEO departures, see Alex Liu, "What Is Ikigai and How Can It Transform Your Leadership and Business for Good?" *World Economic Forum: The Davos Agenda* (January 17, 2022), https://www.weforum.org/agenda/2022/01/ikigai-how-it-can-transform-leadership-and-business-for-good/.

2. The alleged exchange between Fitzgerald and Hemingway (about "the rich" rather than CEOs) is detailed, among other places, in Deirdre N. McCloskey, "'You Know, Ernest, the Rich Are Different from You and Me': A Comment on Clark's *A Farewell to Alms*," *European Review of Economic History* 12, no. 2 (2008): 138–148.

3. For employee happiness and shareholder returns, see, for example, Alex Edmans, Darcy Pu, Chendi Zhang, and Lucius Li, "Employee Satisfaction, Labor Market Flexibility, and Stock Returns Around the World" (January 13, 2023). European Corporate Governance Institute (ECGI) - Finance Working Paper No. 433/2014, Jacobs Levy Equity Management Center for Quantitative Financial Research Paper; Andrew J. Oswald, Eugenio Proto, and Daniel Sgroi, "Happiness and Productivity," *Journal of Labor Economics* 33, no. 4 (2015): 789–822; Christian Krekel, George Ward, and Jan-Emmanuel De Neve, "Happy Employees and Their Impact on Firm Performance," London School of Economics *CentrePiece* (July 15, 2019).

4. For more on skills-based workforce agility, see Neeti Bhardwaj, Steven Berger, Ira Gaberman, and Franziska Neumann, "Focusing on Skills to Win the War for Talent," https://www.kearney.com/leadership-change-organization/article/-/insights/focusing-on-skills-to-win-the-war-for-talent, May 17, 2021.

5. For more on employee value propositions, see Neeti Bhardwaj, Ira Gaberman, and Preethi Prasad, "The New Era of Work Calls for a Next-Level Employee Value Proposition," https://www.kearney.com/leadership-change-organization/article/-/insights/the-new-era-of-work-calls-for-a-next-level-employee-value-proposition, May 3, 2022.

6. For more on effectively leading employees, see Neeti Bhardwaj, Steven Berger, Nigel Andrade, and Ira Gaberman, "Connecting People to Purpose," https://www.kearney.com/leadership-change-organization/article/-/insights/connecting-people-to-purpose, February 10, 2022; Markus Vejvar, "Davos 23 Reflection—Why We (Also) Need a Push from the Middle," *LinkedIn Pulse* (January 31, 2023), https://www.linkedin.com/pulse/davos-23-reflection-why-we-also-need-push-from-middle-markus-vejvar/; Liu, "What Is Ikigai and How Can It Transform Your Leadership and Business for Good?"

7. For more on the purpose gap, including the Polman quote, see Alex Liu and Abby Klanecky, "Overcoming the Purpose Gap: Why There's a Muddle in the Middle," https://www.kearney.com/article/-/insights/overcoming-the-purpose-gap-why-theres-a-muddle-in-the-middle, October 13, 2021.

8. For more on the power of purpose, including sources for these claims, see Alex Liu, Abby Klanecky, and Matt Lubelczyk, "Mission, Metrics, or Somewhere in Between: Where Exactly Does the Purpose Gap Begin?" https://www.kearney.com/article/-/insights/mission-metrics-or-somewhere-in-between-where-exactly-does-the-purpose-gap-begin, June 23, 2021.

9. For more on failures to implement purpose, see the Kearney paper, "55% of Companies Have Yet to Fully Embed Purpose into Their Business," https://www.kearney.com/article/-/insights/55-percent-of-companies-have-yet-to-fuly-embed-purpose-into-their-business, September 22, 2021.

10. For more on the differences in perceived purpose between CXOs and other employees, see Liu, Klanecky, and Lubelczyk, "Mission, Metrics, or Somewhere in Between."

11. For more on the joy gap, see Alex Liu, *Joy Works: Empowering Teams in the New Era of Work* (New York: Wiley, 2022), pp. 23–26.

12. For more on the difference between purpose and leaders' narratives about purpose, see Alex Liu, *Joy Works*, pp. 5–59, 84; Alex Liu's comments at the Bloomberg Live event "Reinvigorating Corporate Purpose," https://www.bloomberglive.com/blog/event-highlights-reinvigorating-corporate-purpose-nov30/, November 30, 2021.

13. For more on embedding a net-zero culture across an organization, see Soon Ghee Chua, Keat Yap, Young Han Koh, and Junru Li, "How to Make Real Progress on the Path to Net Zero," https://www.kearney.com/sustainability/article/-/insights/how-to-make-real-progress-on-the-path-to-net-zero, January 10, 2023.

14. For more on Kearney's views of gamification, see Nigel Andrade, Shannon Warner, Katherine Black, and Ben Bond, "Modernizing Loyalty: So Much More Than Points and Plastic," https://www.kearney.com/consumer-retail/article/-/insights/modernizing-loyalty-so-much-more-than-points-and-plastic, October 7, 2022.

15. For more on the benefits of being a learning organization, see Neeti Bhardwaj, Steven Berger, Ira Gaberman, and Dominique Harris, "Why the Time Is Now to Become a Learning Organization," https://www.kearney.com/leadership-change-organization/article/-/insights/why-the-time-is-now-to-become-a-learning-organization, November 4, 2021.

16. For more on intergenerational learning styles, see the Kearney-Egon Zehnder report "Different Generations, Same Ideals: What Workers of All Ages Value in Their Jobs" (2022), https://www.egonzehnder.com/different-generations-same-ideals, especially pp. 50–54.

17. For more on how to become a learning organization, see Neeti Bhardwaj, Steven Berger, Dominique Harris, and Ira Gaberman, "Making the Move to Become a Learning Organization," https://www.kearey.com/leadership-change-organization/article/-/insights/making-the-move-to-become-a-learning-organization, June 1, 2022.

18. For more on DEI in learning organizations, see Ramyani Basu et al., "Building Back Better for Women at Work," https://www.kearney.com/about/diversity-equity-and-inclusion/women-at-kearney/article/-/insights/building-back-better-for-women-at-work, September 28, 2022.

19. For more on the challenges of logistics, see Anna Kraft, Erin Lai, and Mitchell Nikitin, "How Much Do Customers Really Care About Two-Day Shipping?" https://www.kearney.com/operations-performance-transformation/article/-/insights/how-much-do-customers-really-care-about-two-day-shipping, December 19, 2022.

# Chapter 5  Principle 4

1. For more on the strategic value of warehouses, see Suketu Gandhi, Mihir Tamhankar, and Brittany Cohen, "Warehouses: Hidden in Plain Sight," https://www.kearney.com/operations-performance-transformation/article/-/insights/warehouses-hidden-in-plain-sight, June 28, 2022.

2. For more on technology in warehouses, see the annual *State of Logistics* report, authored by the Council of Supply Chain Management Professionals (CSCMP) with Kearney, especially for the years 2022, 2021, and 2020, at https://cscmp.org/CSCMP/Research/Reports_and_Surveys/State_of_Logistics_Report/CSCMP/Educate/State_of_Logistics_Report.aspx, accessed January 3, 2023.

3. For additional perspectives on warehousing, see the Kearney reports "A Fresh Look: Perishable Supply Chains Go Digital," https://www.kearney.com/operations-performance-transformation/article/-/insights/a-fresh-look-perishable-supply-chains-go-digital, April 16, 2018; "Warehousing: Charting the Way to a Winning Strategy," https://www.kearney.com/operations-performance-transformation/article/-/insights/warehousing-charting-the-way-to-a-winning-strategy, March 17, 2017.

4. For more on Nike and RFID tags, see Sara Silver, "How Kellogg's, Nike, and HP Handled 2020 Supply Chain Disruptions," *Financial Management* (January 25, 2021).

5. For more on Maersk's drones, see Ned Calder, Alasdair Trotter, Conor Carlucci, and Erez Agmoni, "How Maersk Designed a More Resilient Supply Chain," *Harvard Business Review* (November 17, 2022).

6. For more on blockchain in logistics, see the annual *State of Logistics* report, authored by the Council of Supply Chain Management Professionals (CSCMP) with Kearney, especially for the years 2020 and 2019, at https://cscmp.org/CSCMP/Research/Reports_and_Surveys/State_of_Logistics_Report/CSCMP/Educate/State_of_Logistics_Report.aspx, accessed January 3, 2023.

7. For more on the Walmart Canada blockchain, see Kate Vitasek, John Bayliss, Loudon Owen, and Neeraj Srivastava, "How Walmart Canada Uses Blockchain to Solve Supply-Chain Challenges," *Harvard Business Review* (January 5, 2022).

8. For more on SKF Axios, see https://www.skf.com/us/news-and-events/news/2022/2022-05-30-skf-announces-launch-of-skf-axios-powered-by-aws, accessed January 23, 2023.

9. For more on the Siemens Factory of the Year, see "Siemens Factory in Switzerland Wins Award for Production and Supply Chain Resilience," https://press.siemens.com/global/en/pressrelease/siemens-factory-switzerland-wins-award-production-and-supply-chain-resilience, December 15, 2022.

10. For more on the five technologies shaping the future of production, see Xavier Mesnard, "Technology and Innovation for the Future of Production: Accelerating Value Creation," https://www.kearney.com/operations-performance-transformation/article/-/insights/technology-and-innovation-for-the-future-of-production-accelerating-value-creation-article, March 9, 2020. See also Marc Lakner, Ben T. Smith IV, Sebastian Schoemann, Arndt Heinrich, Guido Hertel, and Philip Wessely, "How Is the Fourth Industrial Revolution Changing the Landscape of Manufacturing?" https://www.kearney.com/operations-performance-transformation/article/-/insights/how-is-the-fourth-industrial-revolution-changing-the-landscape-of-manufacturing, February 7, 2020.

11. For more on Airbnb's bold decision, see Adam Dixon, "Setting a Bold Course for Leaders," https://www.kearney.com/leadership-change-organization/article/-/insights/setting-a-bold-course-for-leaders, October 18, 2020.

12. For more on automation and resilience, see Suketu Gandhi, "Leveraging New Tech to Boost Supply Chain Resilience," *Harvard Business Review* (October 26, 2022), https://hbr.org/2022/10/leveraging-new-tech-to-boost-supply-chain-resilience.

13. For more on cobots and the value of humans, including the Kearney/Drishti survey, see Bharat Kapoor, "The State of Human Factory Analytics," https://www.kearney.com/digital/the-state-of-human-factory-analytics, accessed January 9, 2022.

14. For more on the benefits and pitfalls of implementing AI, see Soon Ghee Chua and Nikolai Dobberstein, "Racing Toward the Future: Artificial Intelligence in Southeast Asia," https://www.kearney.com/digital/article/-/insights/racing-toward-the-future-artificial-intelligence-in-southeast-asia, October 7, 2020.

# Chapter 6  Principle 5

1. For the record, SBTs are science-based targets for reduction of greenhouse gases. COP26 is the 2021 United Nations Climate Change Conference in Glasgow, the 26th annual "conference of the parties." GRI is the Global Reporting Initiative, a framework for reporting sustainability progress. SDGs are sustainable development goals, the vehicle and road map for achieving the targets of the COP21 Paris Agreement. See Martin Eisenhut, Michael Strohmer, Imran Dassu, Richard Forrest, and Angela Hultberg, *The Sustainability Chessboard: A New Philosophy of Future Leadership* (Munich: SZ Scala GmbH, 2022), Chapter 2.

2. For customer willingness to pay for sustainability, see Nigel Andrade, Viv Ronnebeck, and Peter Munro, "ESG: A Worthwhile Investment," https://www.kearney.com/sustainability/article/-/insights/esg-a-worthwhile-investment, April 27, 2022; Christina Carlson, Corey Chafin, and Greg Portell, "Consumer Support Still Strong as Earth Day Celebrates Its 50th Birthday," https://www.kearney.com/covid-19/article/-/insights/consumer-support-still-strong-as-earth-day-celebrates-its-50th-birthday, April 21, 2020; Katie Thomas, Angela Hultberg, and Tanya Moryoussef, "Closing the Consumer Aspiration Gap," https://www.kearney.com/consumer-retail/article/-/insights/closing-the-consumer-aspiration-gap, June 23, 2022.

3. For a talent-driven approach to ESG, see Dominique Harris, Karina Toy, Samantha Cochrane, and Emily Murphy, "Your People Will Lead Your Company to Its ESG goals," https://www.kearney.com/leadership-change-organization/article/-/insights/your-people-will-lead-your-company-to-its-esg-goals, October 21, 2022.

4. For a capital markets–driven approach to ESG, see Pablo Moliner Szapáry, Eugenio Prieto Ibanez, Céline Bak, and Javier González, "The ESG Value and Leadership Index," https://www.kearney.com/sustainability/article/-/insights/the-esg-value-and-leadership-index, November 2, 2021.

5. For details on chemical industry scope 3 emissions, including global estimates of propylene emissions by feedstock, see Kish Khemani, Andrew Walberer, Sachidanand

Sahoo, and Colin Etienne, "How Chemical Companies Can Reduce Scope 3 Emissions Now," https://www.kearney.com/chemicals/article/-/insights/how-chemical-companies-can-reduce-scope-3-emissions-now, July 11, 2022.

6. For more on the distinction between *sustainability* strategies and *sustainable* strategies, see Kate Hart, Alasdair Johnston, and Dhananjay Bajaj, "Climate Change: Is Your Organisation Looking at Only One Side of the Coin?" https://www.au.kearney.com/article/-/insights/climate-change-is-your-organisation-looking-at-only-one-side-of-the-coin, August 19, 2022.

7. For more on the Coca-Cola supplier diversity study, see Alexis Bateman, Ashley Barrington, and Katie Date, "Why You Need a Supplier-Diversity Program," *Harvard Business Review* (August 17, 2020).

8. Eisenhut, Strohmer, Dassu, Forrest, and Hultberg, *The Sustainability Chessboard*.

9. For more on scope 3 emissions strategies, see Kish Khemani, Imran Dassu, Evangeline Philos, and Karina Toy, "Scope 3 Emissions Strategy: Why, What, and How," https://www.kearney.com/operations-performance-transformation/article/-/insights/scope-3-emissions-strategy-why-what-and-how, April 20, 2022.

10. For more on secondhand fashion, see Victor Graf Dijon von Monteton and Sabine Spittler, "Think Twice: Why Fashion Brands Should Embrace the Secondhand Opportunity," https://www.kearney.com/consumer-retail/article/-/insights/think-twice-why-fashion-brands-should-embrace-the-secondhand-opportunity, March 10, 2021.

11. For more on CFX and circularity in the fashion industry, see Brian Ehrig, Faycal Baddou, Dario Minutella, and Frederic Dittmar, "The Kearney CFX 2022 Report: Are Fashion Brands Ramping Up Their Circularity Game?" https://www.kearney.com/consumer-retail/article/-/insights/the-kearney-cfx-2022-report-are-fashion-brands-ramping-up-their-circularity-game, April 19, 2022; Mirko Warschun, Saskia God, and Frederic Dittmar, "Can Circularity Save the Fashion Industry?" https://www.nl.kearney.com/consumer-retail/article/-/insights/can-circularity-save-the-fashion-industry, December 3, 2020.

12. For more on supply chain digital twins, see Ben T. Smith IV and P. S. Subramaniam, "How Are Supply Chain Platforms Integrating with AI and Other Advanced Technologies?" https://www.kearney.com/operations-performance-transformation/article/-/insights/how-does-supply-chain-platforms-integrating-with-ai-and-other-advanced-technologies, March 5, 2021.

13. For more on sustainability in design, see the Kearney white papers, "Designing for Sustainability," https://www.kearney.com/product-design-data-platforms/product-excellence-and-renewal-lab/article/-/insights/designing-for-sustainability, December 2, 2021; "When Will Sustainable Design Simply Be Design?" https://www.kearney.com/operations-performance-transformation/article/-/insights/when-will-sustainable-design-simply-be-design, July 20, 2020. For the 2022 survey of consumer sustainability beliefs, see Katie Thomas, Angela Hultberg,

and Tanya Moryoussef, "Closing the Consumer Aspiration Gap," https://www
.kearney.com/consumer-retail/article/-/insights/closing-the-consumer-
aspiration-gap, June 23, 2022.

14. For more on circularity, including the circularity survey, see the Kearney white
paper, "How Do You Move from Laggard to Leader in the Circular Economy?"
https://www.kearney.com/energy/article/-/insights/how-do-you-move-from-
laggard-to-leader-in-the-circular-economy, February 7, 2021.

# Chapter 8  Build Resilience Against Supply Shocks by Working with Supplier Ecosystems

1. For more on sourceability, see Dieter Gerdemann, Michael F. Strohmer, Dominik Leisinger, and Tobias Albers, "Design for Sourcing: How Engineering-Driven Companies
Can Escape the Monopoly Trap," https://www.kearney.com/operations-performance-
transformation/article/-/insights/design-for-sourcing-how-engineering-driven-
companies-can-escape-the-monopoly-trap, November 5, 2021.

2. For more on Coyote Enterprises, see Ian Frazier, *Coyote v Acme* (New York: Farrar,
Straus and Giroux, 2002).

3. For supply resilience advice by industry, see the Kearney paper, "7 Philosophies for
Supply Chain Resilience," https://www.kearney.com/operations-performance-
transformation/article/-/insights/7-philosophies-for-supply-chain-resilience, January 24, 2023.

4. For more on Harry Child, see John Clayton, *Wonderlandscape: Yellowstone National
Park and the Evolution of an American Cultural Icon* (New York: Pegasus, 2017),
pp. 40–44.

5. For more on the German Supply Chain Due Diligence Act, see https://www
.loc.gov/item/global-legal-monitor/2021-08-17/germany-new-law-obligates-
companies-to-establish-due-diligence-procedures-in-global-supply-chains-to-
safeguard-human-rights-and-the-environment/, accessed January 14, 2023.

# Chapter 9  Build Resilience Against Demand Shocks by Operating for the Customer

1. For more on customer intimacy in beauty brands, see the Kearney paper, "Supply
Chains to Embrace the Sharing Economy," https://www.kearney.com/consumer-
retail/article/-/insights/supply-chains-to-embrace-the-sharing-economy,
December 4, 2020.

2. For more on how consumers research and learn, see Katie Thomas, "Reconsidering  Consumer  Education,"  https://www.kearney.com/consumer-retail/

article/-/insights/reconsidering-consumer-education-kearney-consumer-institute-2022-q1-quarterly-brief, February 14, 2022.

3. For more on demand sensing models, see Suketu Gandhi, Bharath Thota, Stuart Klein, and Marc Palazzolo, "Modern Retail Requires Modern Demand Sensing," https://www.kearney.com/analytics/article/-/insights/modern-retail-requires-modern-demand-sensing, January 20, 2023.

4. For more on Arçelik, see World Economic Forum (in collaboration with Kearney), "A Global Rewiring: Redefining Global Value Chains for the Future," https://www3.weforum.org/docs/WEF_A_Global_Rewiring_Global_Value_Chains_2022.pdf, January 2023, p. 14.

5. For more on consumer perceptions of quality, see Katie Thomas and Tanya Moryoussef, "The Death of Price/Value and Dissection of Quality," https://www.kearney.com/consumer-retail/article/-/insights/the-death-of-price-value-and-dissection-of-quality, August 16, 2022.

6. For more on consumers and convenience, see Katie Thomas, "Deconstructing Consumer Convenience," https://www.kearney.com/consumer-retail/article/-/insights/easy-like-sunday-morning-kci-quarterly-briefing-q3-2021, August 13, 2021.

7. For more on Unox ovens, see the Amazon Web Services case study, "UNOX Meets 95% of Service-Level Customer Requests, Drives Innovation by Going All In on AWS," https://aws.amazon.com/solutions/case-studies/unox/, accessed February 8, 2023.

8. For more on Greybull Valley Produce, see Nathan Oster, "Greybull River Produce Flourishing in New Business Park," *Greybull* [Wyo.] *Standard* (March 11, 2021).

9. For more on toilet paper shortages, see Will Oremus, "What Everyone's Getting Wrong About the Toilet Paper Shortage," *Marker/Medium* (April 2, 2020).

10. For more on the pitfalls of omnichannel supply chains, see the Kearney white paper, "Retail: The Omnichannel Supply Chain," https://www.kearney.com/consumer-retail/article/-/insights/retail-the-omnichannel-supply-chain, June 22, 2020.

11. For more on The Home Depot, Kroger, and other retailers' omnichannel strategies, see Jeff Sexstone, Ingo Schroeter, and Marc Palazzolo, "Great Expectations: Delivering on Customer Experience and Fulfillment Profitability," *Supply Chain Management Review* (November 2, 2022), https://www.scmr.com/article/great_expectations_delivering_on_customer_experience_and_fulfillment_profit.

# Chapter 10 Create Resilient Teams by Combining Expertise into Economies of Skill

1. For more on women, DEI, and post-pandemic working conditions, see Ramyani Basu et al., "Building Back Better for Women at Work," https://www.kearney.com/about/diversity-equity-and-inclusion/women-at-kearney/article/-/insights/building-back-better-for-women-at-work, September 28, 2022.

2. For more on DEI listening at Stitch Fix, see Ramyani Basu et al., "Building Back Better for Women at Work."

3. For more on Charlene Thomas's experiences at UPS, see her foreword in Alex Liu, *Joy Works: Empowering Teams in the New Era of Work* (New York: Wiley, 2022), pp. xv–xvii.

4. For more on Tom Kearney, see "Our Founder," https://www.kearney.com/about-kearney/article/-/insights/about-our-founder-article, June 1, 2017.

5. For more on the factors affecting the future work landscape, see the white paper from Kearney and the Misk Global Forum, "Readiness for the Future of Work," https://www.kearney.com/documents/3677458/3679955/READINESS+FOR +THE+FUTURE+OF+WORK.pdf/, March 2019.

6. For more on the characteristics of future ways of working, see Steven Berger, Neeti Bhardwaj, Delphine Bourrilly, and Manale El Kareh, "A Glimpse into the Future of Work," https://www.kearney.com/leadership-change-organization/article/-/ insights/a-glimpse-into-the-future-of-work, October 26, 2022.

7. For more on the Bank of Ireland's Careers Lab and other companies' innovative curriculum options, see Ramyani Basu et al., "Building Back Better for Women at Work."

8. For more on snackable content, see Berger, Bhardwaj, Bourrilly, and El Kareh, "A Glimpse into the Future of Work."

9. For more on agricultural silos, see "History of the Silo," https://silo.org/about-us/ history/history-of-tower-silo/. For more on silos in business, see Caitlin O'Keefe, Nick Anderson, and Will Shalosky, "Siloed Initiatives = Spooked Shareholders: Why Your Supply Chain Must Transform E2E," https://www.kearney.com/operations-performance-transformation/article/-/insights/siloed-initiatives-spooked-shareholders-why-your-supply-chain-must-transform-e2e, October 28, 2022.

## Chapter 11  Combine Human and Artificial Intelligence to Build Resilience Through Constant Learning

1. For more on flywheels, see Jim Collins, *Good to Great: Why Some Companies Make the Leap . . . and Others Don't* (New York: HarperCollins, 2001); Jim Collins, *Turning the Flywheel: A Monograph to Accompany Good to Great* (New York: HarperCollins, 2019). A quick summary is Adewale Adisa, "What Is The Flywheel Effect," *LinkedIn Pulse* (June 16, 2020).

2. For more on procurement analytics, see Elouise Epstein, "Nearly Everything You've Been Told About Procurement Analytics Is Wrong," https://www.kearney.com/procurement/ article/-/insights/nearly-everything-you-ve-been-told-about-procurement-analytics-

is-wrong, May 7, 2019; Elouise Epstein, *Trade Wars, Pandemics, and Chaos: How Digital Procurement Enables Business Success in a Disordered World* (Chicago: Kearney, 2021).

3. For more on AI as a CxO and board-level issue, see Suketu Gandhi and Alanna Klassen Jamjoum, "SAFEguarding AI's trillion-Dollar Opportunity," https://www.kearney.com/digital/article/-/insights/safeguarding-ai-trillion-dollar-opportunity, August 19, 2021.

4. For more on event-driven architecture, see Suketu Gandhi and Jeff Greer, "Transform Your Supply Chain with Event-Driven Architecture," https://www.kearney.com/operations-performance-transformation/article/-/insights/transform-your-supply-chain-with-event-driven-architecture, May 25, 2022.

5. For more on data mesh transformations, see Ramyani Basu, Bharath Thota, and Glyn Heatley, "Delivering Data-as-a-Product," https://www.kearney.com/digital/delivering-data-as-a-product, accessed January 26, 2023.

6. For more on good data practices, see Ujwal Kayande, Enrico Rizzon, and Mohit Khandelwal, "The Impact of Analytics in 2020," https://www.kearney.com/analytics/article/-/insights/the-impact-of-analytics-in-2020, December 1, 2020.

7. For more on Heineken's data initiative, watch the videotaped breakout session "Heineken Brews a New Connected Manufacturing Business" from the AWS re: Invent 2022 conference, https://www.youtube.com/watch?v=liMA7WabMlE&t=2s, December 6, 2022.

8. For more on the Internet of Cows, see Ryan Daws, "Internet of Cows: Ingestible IoT sensor monitors the health of livestock," *Internet of Things News* (November 2, 2021).

9. For more on data integration in manufacturing, see Vidisha Suman and Steven Berger, "How Do We Address the Challenges in Integrating Robotics Data with Operational and Enterprise Systems?" https://www.kearney.com/operations-performance-transformation/article/-/insights/how-do-we-address-the-challenges-in-integrating-robotics-data-with-operational-and-enterprise-systems, March 27, 2020.

10. This is an example of event-driven architecture, as described in Suketu Gandhi and Jeff Greer, "Transform Your Supply Chain with Event-Driven Architecture," https://www.kearney.com/operations-performance-transformation/article/-/insights/transform-your-supply-chain-with-event-driven-architecture, May 25, 2022.

11. For more on DePuy Synthes, see World Economic Forum (in collaboration with Kearney), *Charting the Course for Global Value Chain Resilience* (January 2022), https://www3.weforum.org/docs/WEF_Charting_the_Course_for_Global_Value_Chain_Resilience_2022.pdf: 23; R. Capra et al., "Optimizing Surgical Instrumentation in Orthopedic Surgery: Single Center," *Medicine* 98, no. 7 (2019); the Johnson & Johnson case study at https://www.jnjmedtech.com/en-US/service-details/acm, accessed January 28, 2023.

12. "I Love Lucy: Job Switching," dir. William Asher, written by Jess Oppenheimer, Madelyn Davis, and Bob Carroll Jr. (September 15, 1952).

13. For more on the data-insight-automation progression, see Daniel Angelucci, J. P. Morgenthal, Eric Stettler, and Pablo Escutia Lopez, "Transformative Technologies: Business Process Automation," https://www.kearney.com/digital/transformative-technologies-business-process-automation, accessed January 28, 2023.

14. For more on Rivian, see the Amazon Web Services case study "Rivian Executes Vision of Agile Engineering on AWS," https://aws.amazon.com/solutions/case-studies/rivian-case-study/, accessed January 29, 2023. Disclosure: Rivian also has a partnership with Kearney; see https://www.kearney.com/automotive/article/-/insights/polestar-and-rivian-pathway-report.

# Chapter 12 Ensure Long-Term Resilience by Embracing Sustainability

1. For more on the 100-billion-tonne problem of waste, see the Kearney paper, "Think Fast and Fix Things," https://www.kearney.com/-/insights/think-fast-and-fix-things, December 2, 2021.

2. For more on waste and plastics, see the Kearney paper, "The American Plastic Imperative," https://www.kearney.com/operations-performance-transformation/article/-/insights/the-american-plastic-imperative, December 9, 2020. For details on pandemic-fueled increases in plastic waste, see Monika Kumar, Nina Tsydenova, and Pawan Patil, "Unmasking the Pandemic's Impact on Plastics Waste Management Across South Asia," *World Bank Blogs* (December 13, 2021).

3. For more on consumers' sustainability choices, see Katie Thomas, Angela Hultberg, and Tanya Moryoussef, "Closing the Consumer Aspiration Gap," https://www.kearney.com/consumer-retail/article/-/insights/closing-the-consumer-aspiration-gap, June 23, 2022.

4. For more on Merck's Sustainable Business Value tool, see Eisenhut et al., *The Sustainability Chessboard: A New Philosophy of Future Leadership* (Munich: SZ Scala GmbH, 2022): 59; Herwig Buchholz, Thomas Eberle, Manfred Klevesath, Alexandra Jürgens, Douglas Beal, Alexander Baic, and Joanna Radeke "Forward Thinking for Sustainable Business Value: A New Method for Impact Valuation," *Sustainability* 12, no. 20 (2020): 8420. https://doi.org/10.3390/su12208420.

5. For PepsiCo's data governance, see https://www.pepsico.com/our-impact/esg-topics-a-z/esg-data-governance, accessed January 22, 2023. For context on why it's valuable, see Eisenhut et al., *The Sustainability Chessboard*, pp. 57–58.

6. For more on Alcoa's compensation plan, see Eisenhut et al., *The Sustainability Chessboard*, p. 81.

7. For more on sustainable DEI as a decision metric, see Preethi Prasad and Dominique Harris, "Unapologetically DEI: Designing Equity and Inclusion into the New Era of Work," https://www.kearney.com/leadership-change-organization/article/-/insights/unapologetically-dei-designing-equity-and-inclusion-into-the-new-era-of-work, May 7, 2021.

8. For more on how to market sustainability to consumers, see Katie Thomas, "Reconsidering Consumer Education," https://www.kearney.com/consumer-retail/article/-/insights/reconsidering-consumer-education-kearney-consumer-institute-2022-q1-quarterly-brief, February 14, 2022.

9. For more on why and how to incorporate sustainability into decision-making, see Martin Eisenhut, "Charting a Path to Becoming a Sustainability Leader," *LinkedIn Pulse* (August 30, 2022), https://www.linkedin.com/pulse/charting-path-becoming-sustainability-leader-martin-eisenhut/; Martin Eisenhut, "Seven Steps on the Sustainability Journey," *LinkedIn Pulse* (September 13, 2022), https://www.linkedin.com/pulse/seven-steps-sustainability-journey-martin-eisenhut/.

10. For more on data-driven DEI strategies, see Asha Nooh, Kimberly Bennett, and Silja Baller, "Why Better Reporting on Racial and Ethnic Equity Can Improve Diversity and Inclusion Outcomes," World Economic Forum Annual Meeting, January 23, 2023.

11. For more on DEI accountability methodologies, see Preethi Prasad, Douglas Sandy MacKenzie, Dominique Harris, and Kristen Robinson, "Closing the Corporate Equity Gap: How to Elevate More Women and People of Color in Leadership," https://www.kearney.com/leadership-change-organization/article/-/insights/closing-the-corporate-equity-gap-how-to-elevate-more-women-and-people-of-color-in-leadership, June 16, 2022.

12. For more on PepsiCo's water stewardship pledge, see Christopher Doering, "PepsiCo Aims to Replenish More Water Than It Consumes by 2030," *FoodDive* (August 19, 2021).

13. For more on moving from waste reduction to productive circularity, see Axel Freyberg, Christophe Firth, and Nicole Keller, "When It's Waste, It's Almost Too Late," https://www.kearney.com/telecommunications/article/-/insights/when-its-waste-its-almost-too-late, January 10, 2023.

14. For more on Veja's repair program and sustainability focus, see Rachel Cernansky, "Inside Veja's Direct Supplier Model and Repairs Push," *Vogue Business* (April 29, 2021).

15. For more on steps toward circularity, see Richard Forrest and Oliver Dudok van Heel, "How Regenerative Business Practices Can Reshape Economies," https://www.kearney.com/sustainability/article/-/insights/how-regenerative-business-practices-can-reshape-economies, January 16, 2023.

16. For more on plastics recycling rates, see Daniel De Visé, "Why Most Plastic Isn't Getting Recycled," *The Hill* (November 1, 2022).

17. For more on plastics recycling, see Rajeev Prabhakar, Andrew Walberer, Kish Khemani, and Emily Rowe, "The Fight for Recycled Feedstock," https://www.kearney.com/sustainability/article/-/insights/the-fight-for-recycled-feedstock, December 21, 2022.

## Chapter 14 Industry Case Studies on How the Principles Can Help in Future Scenarios

1. For more on the future of pharma, including risks of patent expiry, see Marc P. Philipp and Martin Hodosi, "Refueling the Pipeline: How Pharma Can Up the Dose on R&D," https://www.kearney.com/health/article/-/insights/refueling-the-pipeline-how-pharma-can-up-the-dose-on-r-d, June 13, 2022.

2. For more on pharmaceutical supply chains, including geopolitical risks, demand spikes, and how to respond, see Vishal Bhandari, Mike Piccarreta, Pablo Moliner Szapáry, and Rosanna Lim, "Building Resilient Pharma Supply Chains," https://www.kearney.com/health/article/-/insights/three-ways-to-build-resilience-into-pharmaceutical-supply-chains, February 23, 2022.

3. For future pharma trends, including AI, see Todd Huseby and Jeffrey Woldt, "Video Forum: Todd Huseby: Trends Shaping the Healthcare Sector," *Chain Drug Review* (February 13, 2023), https://www.chaindrugreview.com/video-forum-todd-huseby-kearney-2/.

4. For retail pharma trends, including smaller and niche strategies, see Huseby and Woldt, "Video Forum."

5. For more on the implications of integrated care, see Kathryn Rauen, Kate Maheu, and D. J. McKerr, "In the Race to Integrate Care, Will Pharmacies Get Lost in the Shuffle?" https://www.kearney.com/article/-/insights/in-the-race-to-integrate-care-will-pharmacies-get-lost-in-the-shuffle, July 29, 2022. For more on value-based care in the US, see Rodey Wing, Tonny Huang, and Laura Bowen, "Value-Based Care an Opportunity for Rx," *Chain Drug Review* (November 21, 2022).

6. For more on tech supply chains, with a particular focus on semiconductors, see Mike Hales, Danish Faruqui, Dieter Gerdemann, Bharat Kapoor, Hieu Pham, and Archit Johar, "Why a Resilient Semiconductor Supply Chain Is Imperative—and How to Create One," https://www.kearney.com/technology/article/-/insights/why-a-resilient-semiconductor-supply-chain-is-imperative-and-how-to-create-one, May 11, 2021.

7. For tech-enabled customer value propositions, see Mike Chapman, Michael Felice, Amro Messaoudi, and Paul Weichselbaum, "Streaming Providers Need New

Ways to Drive Growth," *Fierce Video* (March 13, 2023), https://www.fiercevideo
.com/video/streaming-providers-need-new-ways-drive-growth-part-2-industry-
voices-chapman.

8.  For more on component shortages and other industrial supply chain issues, see
the Kearney paper, "7 Philosophies for Supply Chain Resilience," https://www
.kearney.com/operations-performance-transformation/article/-/insights/7-
philosophies-for-supply-chain-resilience, January 24, 2023.

9.  For more on resilience in last-mile distribution, see Balika Sonthalia, Rupal
Deshmukh, Marc Palazzolo, and Elise Kerner, "How Can Retailers Build Resilience in Last-Mile Distribution?" https://www.kearney.com/telecommunications/
article/-/insights/how-can-retailers-build-resilience-in-last-mile-distribution,
December 21, 2021; Anna Kraft, Erin Lai, and Mitchell Nikitin, "How Much
Do Customers Really Care About Two-Day Shipping?" https://www.kearney
.com/operations-performance-transformation/article/-/insights/how-much-do-
customers-really-care-about-two-day-shipping, December 19, 2022.

# Chapter 16  Some Questions to Ask Yourself About the Future of Your Operations

1.  For more on the Intel-Brookfield deal, see the Intel press release, "Intel Introduces
First-of-its-Kind Semiconductor Co-Investment Program" (August 23, 2022).

2.  For more on operating models, see Hagen Götz Hastenteufel, Sarah Helm, Luca
Spring, and Adithi Raju, "Countering Complexity: Time to Get the Operating
Model on the Operating Table?" https://www.kearney.com/leadership-change-
organization/article/-/insights/countering-complexity-time-to-get-the-operating-
model-on-the-operating-table, January 27, 2023.

3.  For more on the sustainability chessboard, see Martin Eisenhut, Michael Strohmer,
Imran Dassu, Richard Forrest, and Angela Hultberg, *The Sustainability Chessboard:
A New Philosophy of Future Leadership* (Munich: SZ Scala GmbH, 2022). There's a
free online summary at https://www.kearney.com/sustainability/the-sustainability-
chessboard, accessed March 15, 2023.

4.  Yoda quoted in Jude Watson, *The Mark of the Crown (Star Wars: Jedi Apprentice, Book
4)* (New York: Scholastic, 1999), p. 13.

# ACKNOWLEDGMENTS

We want to extend our deepest thanks to our colleagues and collaborators for their ongoing support. Without your dedication, support, and insights, this book would not have been possible.

We want to particularly thank **Per Hong** for his thought leadership on global value chain reconfiguration and for sharing insights from our partnership on the future of global value chains with the World Economic Forum.

This book draws on the expertise and thought leadership of hundreds of Kearney consultants, many of whom are cited in the notes. In particular, we want to extend our gratitude to the following individuals for their ongoing commitment in making this book what it is.

Thanks to . . .

- Markus Vejvar for managing the publication process from start to finish, ensuring that we met our deadlines and stayed close to our original vision.
- John Clayton for helping us refine our language and maintain a common voice.
- Haley Dunbrack and our global marketing team for supporting us in publishing and marketing this book.
- Alex Liu for his exemplary leadership, his passion and his vision for our firm.
- Geir Olsen for his continuous guidance and dedication to Strategic Operations.
- David Hanfland, Arjun Sethi and Bob Willen for their leadership and their ongoing counsel and support.

- Dominique Harris, Beth Bovis, and our Leadership, Change, and Organization practice for their perspectives on the future of work, diversity and inclusion, and workplace empowerment.
- Bharat Kapoor, Dominik Leisinger, and the PERLab team for providing their insights and many examples from the product design perspective.
- Katie Thomas and the Kearney Consumer Institute team for valuable insights on how to operate for the consumer.
- Rupal Deshmukh and the Kearney Supply Chain Institute team for supporting our vision of the book with their input.
- Our Global Industry practice heads Rhiannon Thomas, John Wolff, Nikolai Dobberstein, and Michael J. Wise for providing feedback and input on the future of operations in their respective industries.
- Daniel Stengel and the Factory of the Year team for the examples "from the shopfloor" that we highlight in this book, most notably, the examples of Rational's supply chain management and the Siemens Smart Factory in Zug.
- Andreas Kaltenbrunner, Maximilian Merklinger, and Saad Farhad for their support in the generation of the initial exposé of this book.
- Tom Adams, Julian L. Morgan, Michel Putnik and Joseph Rosing and their teams at Amazon Web Services for their support.
- Steve Mehltretter, Robert Kromoser, Fabian Siegrist, Gillis Jonk, Tobias Lewe, Marcus Weber, Young Han Koh, and many others who discussed the ideas in this book with us and shared related client experiences.
- Our global strategic operations leadership team who shaped our Kearney knowledge and the experience this book is based on through hundreds of client projects: Mesut Korhan Acar, Rahul Anand, Venky Arun, Jens Behre, John Blascovich, Marina Catino, Jesse R. Chafin, Nithin Chandra, Mark R. Clouse, Ana Conde, Imran Dassu, Remko de Bruijn, Dennis Kip Dowding, William J. Duffy, Chin F. Eng, Kai Engel, Azaz Faruki, John Paul Fiorentino, Benoit Gougeon, Dave Gowans, Prashant Gupta, Patrick Haischer, Nori Hamaguchi, Rob Harriss, Kate Hart, Rene Heller, Sid Jain, Vikas Kaushal, Antti Kautovaara, Arun Kochar, Tomo Kozaki, Oleg Kozyrenko, Remco Kroes, Sumeet Ladsaongikar, Robin Lemke, Brooks A. Levering, Adam Li, Silvana

L. Lischner, Dipankar Maganty, Federico Mariscotti, Andreas Mayer, Marcos Mayo, Sumit Mitra, Sujeet Morar, Shakil Nathoo, Caitlin C O'Keefe, Gaurav Parmar, Jim Pearce, Nigel Pekenc, Hemanth Peyyeti, Jaroslaw Podsiadlo, Philip Rauen, Enzio Reincke, Enrico Rizzon, Ingo Schroeter, Jeff Sexstone, Subramaniam Pazhayanur Shanmukham, John Song, Balika Narendra Sonthalia, Yves Thill, Patrick Van Den Bossche, Jos van Iwaarden, Henning Wachtendorf, Fabrice Wagner, Jane Wanklyn, Philip Wessely, Chee Chiew Wong, Keat Yap, Fabio Eiji Yoshitome, and Michael W Zimmerman.
- At Wiley, Richard Narramore for acquiring the book, Zachary Schisgal for championing it, Venkatasubramanian Chellian for overseeing production, Kristi Bennett for developmental editing, Susan Geraghty for copyediting, Sophia Ho for proofreading.
- All of the clients, colleagues, friends, and partners who have provided feedback and their endorsement of the manuscript.

# ABOUT US

Kearney is a leading global management consulting firm with more than 5,300 people working in more than 40 countries. We work with more than three-quarters of the Fortune Global 500, as well as with the most influential governmental and nonprofit organizations. We are individuals who take as much joy from those we work with as the work itself.

Since 1926, we have been trusted advisors to the world's foremost organizations, and we continue to live by the principles established by our founder Andrew Thomas (Tom) Kearney so long ago: "Our success as consultants will depend on the essential rightness of the advice we give and our capacity for convincing those in authority that it is good."

Kearney is a partner-owned firm with a distinctive, collegial culture that transcends organizational and geographic boundaries. As a firm we strive to be the difference for our clients, our people, and our society. To be the difference for our people, we live by our five core values—curiosity, generosity, boldness, solidarity, and passion. As a result, our consultants are down-to-earth, approachable, and have a shared passion for doing innovative client work that provides clear benefits to the organizations we work with in both the short and long term.

## About the Kearney Supply Chain Institute

Decades ago, Kearney was the original operations consulting firm. Today that legacy continues with the Kearney Supply Chain Institute (KSCI), which generates strategic insights to help global business leaders. KSCI's regular studies and competitions include the annual Kearney Reshoring

Index, the annual *State of Logistics* report, and the Assessment of Excellence in Procurement. Whether the topic is the need for growth, cost improvement, sustainability, or resilience, KSCI unravels global value chain trends to help business leaders undertake their supply chain transformations.

## About Kearney's Collaboration with the World Economic Forum

Kearney's collaboration with what is now the World Economic Forum dates back to 1971. From technology and the environment to inclusion issues and beyond, our collaboration with the Forum community enacts our commitment to improving the state of the world. Our collaboration's recent insights and tools include The Resiliency Compass, a comprehensive framework to help companies understand and prepare for future disruptions.

## About Kearney's Factory of the Year

Since 1992, Kearney has run the Factory of the Year, the world's most rigorous operations assessment for manufacturing companies. More than 2,000 factories—across the automotive, consumer packaged goods (CPG), high tech, mining, and electronics sectors—have used this impartial, cross-industry benchmarking contest to determine their relative position of operational excellence. Performance is assessed along more than 100 benchmarks in dimensions such as value creation, economics, quality, agility, digitization, and sustainability.

## About Kearney's PERLab

Kearney's Product Excellence and Renewal Lab (PERLab) helps clients make the products that customers fall in love with. The design-driven approach to gross margin transformation offers end-to-end capabilities—PERLab can support growth at any point in a product's life cycle. PERLab experts—in product design, product development, sustainability, user experience, industrial design, the Internet of Things (IoT), consumer insights, product engineering, packaging design, and manufacturing excellence—help organizations disrupt markets and leapfrog the competition. PERLab has studios in Chicago, Stuttgart, and Bengaluru. Its clients range from Fortune 500 to private equity portfolio companies.

## About the Kearney Consumer Institute (KCI)

The Kearney Consumer Institute (KCI) evaluates today's business challenges and opportunities through the eyes and experiences of consumers, advocating a consumer-first perspective. With a consumer-first lens, KCI looks at today's consumer revolution by thinking like consumers. By analyzing consumer behavior and insights from around the world, KCI generates conversation about, and ultimately action on, how to address consumer needs with meaningful benefits. KCI's consumer-centric approach includes simple, precise, plain-language conversations on topics such as trends, consumer communities, convenience, loyalty, service, fair pricing, and product development and technologies.

# ABOUT THE AUTHORS

**S**uketu Gandhi is global colead of Kearney's strategic operations practice. Based in the Chicago office, Suketu is a recognized industry leader and subject matter expert on a wide range of operations topics, with an emphasis on end-to-end supply chains. "I'm strongly focused on the redesign of supply chains for four critical purposes: growth, cost, resilience, and sustainability," he comments. "The key to maximizing their effectiveness lies in the combination of human intelligence, AI, and automation, underpinned by a deep understanding of how global operations work."

Suketu's passion for operations work goes back to the earliest days of his career with a major retailer. He quickly realized that supply chains and operational excellence are critical to satisfying customers, and he decided he wanted to master every facet of operations. Now, he puts this knowledge to work for clients throughout the consumer and retail space. In one end-to-end transformation effort, his team helped the client achieve several points of growth coupled with nearly double-digit cost reduction.

Suketu is frequently published on operations transformation topics in outlets such as *Harvard Business Review*, *MIT Sloan Management Review*, and *The Wall Street Journal*.

**Michael F. Strohmer** is an internationally recognized expert in strategic end-to-end operations, procurement transformations, and sustainability. He is Vienna based and joined Kearney in 2001. In his role as global colead for the strategic operations practice and lead for procurement at Kearney, he is the sponsor of the competence team for sustainable sourcing.

Michael has led a range of projects with a broad range of international clients in different geographies, mainly in post-merger integrations and private equity–driven carve-outs. His work is mainly focused on private equity and encompasses consumer/luxury goods, automotive, defense, process industries, and utilities in Europe, Asia, and the United States. As an expert in procurement, he works especially on raw materials, large-scale capex, and disruptive levers in procurement.

Michael is also coauthor of several books, including *The Purchasing Chessboard*, *The CPO*, *Supplier Relationship Management*, and *Disruptive Procurement*. Michael is a trusted advisor for many CxOs on the future of the economy, particularly the future of operations. He lives in Austria's wonderful nature in a village in the mountains.

A Kearney partner with a can-do mentality, **Marc Lakner** develops tailored, mission-critical solutions and supports his clients in the implementation. He is Kearney's managing director for Germany, Austria, and Switzerland and a member of the European leadership team. These roles keep him on the road on behalf of his international clients from the engineered goods industries—be it to develop successful transformation programs, implement ambitious performance improvements, or execute organizational and operational model design projects. Marc is an expert in digital manufacturing, Industry 4.0, supply chain management, and innovative material cost reductions. In addition, he has been global sponsor and host of the Kearney Factory of the Year event for many years.

**Tiffany Hickerson** is a partner in Kearney's strategic operations practice. With more than 20 years of industry and consulting experience, Tiffany is known for leading largescale transformations focused on procurement value capture, ESG, organizational design, and capability building. In addition to helping clients thrive, Tiffany is a highly regarded people leader, ombudsperson, mental health ambassador, and the sponsor of the Black@Kearney affinity group. Tiffany has been recognized by Consulting Magazine as an Emerging Leader in Consulting, as one of Diversity MBA Magazine's Top 100 Under 50 Emerging Leaders, and by Working Mother magazine as Kearney's Working Mother of the Year. Tiffany is based of out the Chicago office and is married and a mother of two boys.

**Sherri (Xiaoqing) He** is the managing director of Kearney's Greater China unit and global partner leading the consumer and retail practice in Greater China. Sherri has more than 20 years of consulting experience. She has served multinational corporate clients and Chinese local clients in consumer goods, retail, private equity, and other industries in China. Sherri's areas of expertise include strategy, digital transformation, e-commerce, new retail, sales and marketing, operation improvement, M&A/PMI, and organization transformation. Sherri was nominated by *Consulting* Magazine for "Excellence in Client Service" at the 2022 Women Leaders Awards.

# INDEX